i

The Ultimate Question: in search of God in a godless universe

By Professor Anthony O'Hear, Honorary Director of the Royal Institute of Philosophy in London

It would be very hard not to find much to agree with, and probably much to disagree with, in Hazhir Teimourian's *The Ultimate Question*. For he is, in the best sense of the word, an engaged thinker. That is, he takes ideas about the most important things seriously. He reads, he thinks, he wrestles. And he draws conclusions. In all of this, his engagement, while rational, is personal, anything but academic in the pejorative sense.

I said that Teimourian reads. He reads in philosophy, in science, in history. He also has a fascinating background, coloured by a near-Zoroastrian Kurdish upbringing and an unquenchable love of Omar Khayyam, who is in some sense Teimourian's lodestone and whom we read here in his own translation.

If critical thinking means anything, Teimourian's wide and deep reading is informed by critical thinking. That is to say, he reads and reasons about what he reads. He is respectful to those he reads, but he does them the honour of taking them seriously enough to disagree.

It would be true to say that there is in Teimourian's make-up a vein of religious scepticism. As a Fellow of the Royal Astronomical Society, he is deeply impressed by the extent and nature of the Universe, as expounded by modern science, and he is only too aware of the problems of evil and suffering. He finds it hard, if not impossible, to accept the idea of a personal God, as expounded in the traditional Abrahamic faiths.

But notwithstanding his religious scepticism, Teimourian is clearly unimpressed by the efforts of some contemporary physicists and cosmologists to explain or explain away the mystery of existence. His exposition of the tangles into which some of the leading figures in this area have become enmeshed is delightfully clear-headed.

For Teimourian the mystery remains, and cannot be solved within science or within the material world. Resorting to the Latin metaphor Ultima Thule for the unattainable dream, he invokes a notion he calls *Ultima* to express what he thinks must lie behind or beyond what we know or can know. This has some of the resonance of the traditional God and might yield some of the benefits of traditional religion. In following him in this quest, there is much to agree with. To disagree with? I am sure that our author would take thoughtful disagreement as a compliment, but if and when we disagree, we should not forget that he has a canny sense of the right questions and also of what really matters.

A History of Philosophy in Mesopotamia, Classical Iran and Early Islam

Hazhir Teimourian

For the long-suffering Yārsāni religious community in the Middle East to whom I once belonged, with gratitude. They have even deeper roots in the history of humanity than I thought I knew.

And for Christabel.

"This Sea of Being has come out of naught.
No glimpse of its truth has anyone caught.
Many a clown has put forth his thought:
From the Other Side news cannot be sought."

Contents

1

Introduction

and acknowledgements

Christians burned many more books than Muslims ever did. Muslims only stopped them being written in the first place!

This work owes its birth to an after-dinner speech delivered at the Royal Society of Medicine in London in late 2023. A group of amateur and professional philosophers, including Adrian Pilkington and Deborah Vorhies, who meet there several times a year, were interested in hearing why, in my opinion, the vast world of Islam had not produced a first-rate philosopher for eight centuries. By "first-rate" here I mean philosophers who are familiar names in philosophy faculties in most parts of the world. There are three such philosophers hailing from the world of Islam. They are Fārābī, Avicenna and Averroes. Their works were translated into Latin and taught at leading centres of learning in medieval Europe for a number of centuries. But even they produced largely only commentaries on Aristotle and were preoccupied by reconciling reason to scriptural cosmogonies. Ever since, despite the West having been open to new ideas from anywhere else in the world, not a single philosopher born and bred in a Muslim land has stamped his mark on mainstream philosophy.

I concluded that the explanation was not wholly the seemingly obvious, that a literalist religion such as Islam would not allow the kind of free speculation in which philosophers thrive. There had been quite a number of enlightened Muslim rulers who had felt secure enough on their thrones for long enough to silence the most strident of their clerics and to enable freethinkers to mature at their courts. A good example was the renowned poet-astronomer of Persia, Omar Khayyām, the first detailed biography of whom I had myself completed some years earlier. As the leading teacher of what they called "the sciences of

3

Yunān" in Isfahān in the late eleventh century, Khayyām was safe as long as his friend and protector, the Saljuq emperor Malik Shah, lived. But when in 1092 the latter was poisoned in Baghdad and the empire fell apart in a dynastic war, the Muslim clergy unveiled their revenge. They issued fatwas of death against Khayyām "for loving the Greeks" and forced him to flee to a safe corner. Nor had Islam been alone in persecuting freethinkers. Christianity, despite proclaiming itself primarily as a religion of forgiveness, has, as we all know, an appalling record of cruelty against sceptics. Yet its dominions have produced virtually all the abstract philosophy of the world since the fall of Rome. We must therefore look for other factors, too, to explain the plight of philosophy among Muslims.

The reception for what I had to say was so enthusiastic that we all agreed, there and then, that I should contemplate writing a longer treatment of the question. Later, however, as I examined my motives and circumstances as the proverbial "old man in a hurry", a man in his ninth decade, I decided that my heart was not in the project. It was a negative enterprise and a vast project. Younger, full-time academics were better placed to look into it.

Instead, I gravitated towards a less opinionated, more historical narrative that covered a longer period and was easier to write. What is usually called the Golden Age of Islam, what we might call Islam's "innocent" early centuries, when many important works of the Greeks and others were translated into Arabic to produce, eventually, the three philosophers just mentioned, did not sprout out of barren earth. Jews and Christians were well established in Muhammad's Mecca before he started his career as a prophet and, for thousands of years previously, the Middle East had been the middle ground of material and intellectual traffic between Asia and Europe and had, moreover, itself produced the origins of writing and arithmetic, geometry and astronomy, as well as works of elaborate engineering, not to

4

mention the great Abrahamic religions of Judaism and Christianity. It had also produced and developed the religion of Zarathustra, Zoroastrianism, a dynamic scene of speculation on ethics, ontology and political philosophy that Plato so admired and which Pliny the Elder described as "the most famous and most useful" in the world. Indeed, perhaps it could not have been otherwise. Agriculture also originated in the Middle East, perhaps over 12,000 years ago, and the surpluses in food and wealth that it produced in a climate of warm summer evenings spent around meals in orchards or by desert camp fires could not fail but make the region prolific in producing new ideas. The world's oldest surviving novel, the Epic of Gilgamesh, which has come down to us largely intact on clay tablets, is a brilliant example and embodies a strong notion of social justice and the philosophy of state. Zoroastrianism, too, with its offshoots such as Mithraism that spread as far west as the Irish Sea, made considerable contributions to Greek religion and philosophy. So it might be useful to widen the area of my enquiry and tell the story of philosophising, as well as proper, formal philosophy, in the region, from Sumer to Andalusia.

A legitimate question arises here: Why do I think that I am placed well enough to write this book? One answer may be that, while certainly far from unique, I am not without a few advantageous or relevant attributes. These include my possessing what I would call "the native's feel" for the languages of the region, from ancient Avestan to today's Kurdish, and the native's life-long curiosity about the lives of his ancestors, plus even a childhood and early manhood of treading in their physical steps, breathing in the air of the same hilltops and bathing in the same rivers. This means, certainly in my case, an enhanced will to understand. Empathy with those long gone surely follows. I am also trained in philosophy and, crucially, keep abreast of the latest physics and astronomy. Important, too, is my having acquired a hand in English.

These are not commonplace characteristics in a commentator. Nor is the unusual religion of my youth with its deep roots in those same ancient times and peoples. I was brought up in the Yārsān religion of Iranian Kurdistan, in particular the province of Kermanshah that formed the very heartland of both ancient Media and Sasanian Iran. I am familiar with the belief system and rites of worship of the Yārsāni people which are rooted in the Zoroastrianism of the Sasanians, above all others, knowledge which has of necessity been hidden from the prying eyes of Muslim states. Though I gave up my inherited creed long ago, I have further studied its doctrines and history in the open and relaxed intellectual space of England. In this respect, a book of these attributes can have been written only by someone who "belonged".

To five philosopher friends I owe debts of gratitude for helping to inform my writing in recent years. They are Peter Cave, John Cottingham, Robert Grant, Anthony O'Hear and Raymond Tallis. I have benefitted enormously from reading their books and the privilege of their company, and most of us have memories of the friendship and greatness of the late Roger Scruton in common. Thus perhaps I ought to mention, also, the debt I owe Roger, who, incidentally, wrote a history of philosophy of his own, a history of modern Philosophy which I find I still consult frequently.

Finally, a note is perhaps apt on why I did not offer this book to traditional publishers. My friend and agent, the renowned Sonia Land of Sheil Land Literary Associates, one of Britain's five largest such agencies, had made it clear to me in recent years that she was not interested in receiving philosophy from me because reputable publishers no-longer published books that lacked a prospect of large sales. As a result, I took advantage of Amazon's Kindle Direct Publishing platform and published the work myself. I was delighted with the experience. I did not have to wait a year for publishers to consider the offering over several months and then, if favourable, place it on their schedule for the following year. Sadly also, as most of my friends in academia complained, even the largest of those publishers no-longer promoted their titles seriously, nor even employed editors to correct typographic errors. Yet another delight was that the book became available to its potential readers all over the world at an affordable price, not at the kind of price that only the richest academic institutions could ponder. A third advantage was that I, the author, did not lose control of the contents the moment I signed the contract. As someone has said so truthfully of old-style publishing, an author's published work will for ever remain his penultimate draft. Errors, big and small, and the need for improvements, will haunt his dreams for the rest of his life and cause him ask himself why he had not waited just a little longer. Thus I intend that, for as long as I can, this offering in your hand will be, not the favourite of its creator's yesterday, but his latest considered opinion.

April 2025
Sussex

<u>ONE</u>

The first 3000 years: from Uruk to Persepolis

The Flood Tablet of the Epic of Gilgamesh in Babylonian – British Museum

Surely, philosophy has always been with us. It is essentially wondering about the world, asking abstract questions, questions that cannot be answered through measurement and the empirical, scientific method. As such, it haunted the minds of our very first human ancestors, perhaps some 200,000 years ago. Around a camp fire after a communal meal somewhere in north-east Africa or the Midde East, a man or a woman asked himself or herself why the world existed at all, whether life, any life, had a purpose, if humans were special? No doubt a little later, the next steps were taken. Someone with a more powerful imagination made up stories hinting at possible answers in order to amuse or impress.

Philosophy as we define it formally today came into being in ancient Greece fairly recently, only some two-and-a-half millennia ago. That is when, as far as we know, some questions at the heart of philosophy were first committed to writing and discussed in formal gatherings of teachers and students. To my mind, though, it is admissible to be flexible, to be less rigid. Can we not see that much writing before Thalis of Miletus, the first designated philosopher, had philosophical assumptions strongly implied in them? Did the myriad societies that are known to us today from ancient Mesopotamia, Egypt and the Sind Valley not have philosophical assumptions of justice and social contracts underpinning their political structures?

If we allow ourselves to be so flexible, we can see that the world's oldest-recorded philosophy of state speaks to us loudly in the Epic of Gilgamesh, the world's oldest discovered literary composition as recorded on clay tablets and found in the ruins of the city of Uruk in ancient southern Iraq. The tablets go back to around 2100 years BC, but the text on them is older. They are copies of a poem that may well have circulated locally for many centuries already. Later versions were compiled and edited in Babylonia and Assyria, further north. But all share a common beginning: Gilgamesh, when young, started his rule over Uruk by abusing his subjects. He demanded of males that they perform unreasonable forced labour for him and, far worse, he entitled himself to the virginity of young women on their wedding nights. So the town's citizens resorted to the gods to rescue them from the tyranny and the gods created Enkidu, a man-like creature with superhuman strength, to overthrow Gilgamesh.

10

Thus can we claim that before Gilgamesh, there had been a custom or convention in Uruk that the ruler and the ruled bore moral obligations towards one another, the origin of the so-called social contract of modern, Western philosophy. Governance was by covenant. In return for taxes and some labour by the able-bodied on public projects, the king behaved with consideration towards his people. As well as protecting them from external threats by maintaining an army, he and his officials abstained from cruelty and avarice. If they failed to live by what was expected of them, they lost legitimacy and those citizens who rose against them became entitled to the backing of civil society and the temples, with the latter's priesthood, indeed, being a powerful force in the land.

In this respect, we may regard the opening lines of the epic as the constitution of the Sumerian monarchy, albeit with some of the shortcomings, as well as the advantages, of today's unwritten British constitution. It is true that, unfortunately for the people of Uruk, Gilgamesh proved stronger than the creature sent down to defeat him, implying that even the gods – metaphors for the forces of nature – were not omnipotent. In fact, the king and the semi-beast became partners, inseparable companions, until the gods changed their minds and killed Enkidu for disobedience. But at least the story no-longer mentions any crimes committed against the people by the two. Instead, they devote their energies to discovering the secret of eternal life until, towards the end, Gilgamesh becomes a "wise man". A later editor re-titled the epic "He Who Saw into the Deep" and gifted the world with its first "philosopher king", for Gilgamesh learned from the follies of his youth and concluded that, in fact, eternal life would be a calamity.

We may say, of course, that this primitive, indirectly-expressed thesis for a stable state was not, at the time, confined to Uruk, that it has been understood by all human societies since our

11

earliest days. This is because coercion is not conducive to smooth cooperation and that, sooner or later, the frictions and resentments that hidden strife causes will weaken the state and lay it open to threats from within and without. Voluntary consensus, willing cooperation, is much more efficient in uniting the resources of a polity against those who wish it ill. But what is significant in the case of Uruk is that the understanding attained widespread recognition when it was inserted into a popular tale over 4000 years ago. Nor does it detract from the importance of the achievement that this early instance of idealism has in subsequent ages been more often violated than honoured. It remains a proud and telling part of the vast heritage of Mesopotamia and became a model of good conduct expected of rulers for countless generations afterwards.

If this analysis is justified, we can try to imagine how the unwritten covenant might have arisen. Uruk began as a small village by the estuary of the Euphrates soon after the last ice age. Its inhabitants, probably numbering only a dozen or so households, lived by fishing, herding cattle and buffaloes in the marshes, nursing fruit trees, and cultivating some grains on higher ground. They belonged, in all probability, to a single extended family and everyone knew everyone else. Bullying or injustice were too disruptive to be tolerated by the clan's elders. Thus, as supported by extensive archaeological research, Uruk grew steadily in prosperity and population and began to trade with other, similar communities nearby. In a millennium or two, it became the capital city of the region, the region of Sumer, whose people are thought to have been related to those of the Indus Valley in today's Pakistan. Whatever the precise combination of factors, though, it proved one of the most successful in world history. Uruk's gods became revered widely and its priests simplified their initial pictographs into wedge-shaped "cuneiform" letters to devise Humanity's first, comprehensive recorder of speech. Such was Uruk's eventual standing far and wide that when, thousands of years later, it was conquered by the Semitic-speaking Babylonians in the north, the conquerors adopted its language as their lingua franca and used it for ages as the sacred liturgical language of their temples. Even today, whenever we hear the name of the modern state of Iraq, Uruk, Biblical Erekh, resonates in our ears[1].

***

A distinct deterioration in Mesopotamian politics may be seen in the famous legal code of Hammurabi, the sixth Amorite ruler of Babylon in the 18th century BC. To begin with, the long document delights the eye with its familiar literary structure. It has a preface, a main body and an epilogue. It is clearly the work of an experienced editor, the leader of a team of speech writers and legal officials who spent years huddled in committees shaping their collection and ironing out impracticalities, inconsistencies and duplications. On closer inspection, however, we see how distant it is from the mutual considerations that informed the Gilgamesh tail of Uruk. It is boastful in the extreme, for it is the command of a king who is in daily contact with the gods, especially the Sun and the Moon, if not depicting himself quite at their level, for he says that he prostrates himself in adulation of them daily. This law, he says, was given to him by Shamash – the Sun, who is also the god of wisdom – and Marduk, the supreme deity of Babylon and the mighty god of justice. In the same vein, Hammurabi proclaims his reverence for the deities of all the major centres of population under his rule, including Uruk and Assur, and reminds their inhabitants of the treasures he has spent on enhancing their temples and public amenities, even of the help he gives to the poor. Then he lays

---

[1] By way of Middle Persian, which pronounced Uruk as Erāq.

13

before them his 282 decrees, each stipulating a specific punishment for a specific crime.

Hammurabi's law is harsh, as is probably to be expected in an honour-bound society. An eye is to be gouged out in return for the crime of the same kind, as is a tooth for a tooth – lex talionis in Latin. But Hammurabi goes further. The crimes of the fathers will be visited on their children. If, for example, a murderer dies before he receives his just retribution, his eldest son will be executed in his place. We can envisage the unhappiness of many a wiser head among the populace who would deem the act unjust. But all initiative, any interpretation that is not in line with the strict letter of his law, is forbidden. The sparsity of political wisdom here is also perhaps surprising. Some of the towns and cities that Hammurabi had conquered recently had their own customary practices and legal histories. All are now commanded to implement the law of Babylon.

Hammurabi is particularly brutal to women. He gives their husbands almost total power over them, to the extent that the men are commanded to "throw them into the river" if they are caught having an illicit affair. Only when he remembers that most women have fathers and brothers, does he make modest amendments to the law. He says that if a woman can prove before a law court that her husband has maltreated her, she is allowed to leave him and take her dowry with her.

To be fair, if the punishments are harsh, so are the standards of proof demanded. Would-be accusers are warned that, should they later be found to have lied, their punishment will be more severe than what they caused to be inflicted on their victims. Thus it is likely that most men thought twice before they placed a complaint before a judge.

Reading the whole document, the thought occurs to one that Hammurabi, mighty ruler and demigod, as he was, may have harboured in his heart the fear that he was not loved by the majority of the peoples over whom he wielded suzerainty, and that rebellion could be raised suddenly somewhere. He craves popularity. He has issued the code, he says, "to punish the wicked and protect the weak from the strong". This would have resonated with some, perhaps mostly in the provinces, who had previously lived under cruel or avaricious local masters. The same would apply to isolated communities that had been practically without a legal code of their own. So Hammurabi insists on his decrees being brought to widespread public notice. They must be chiselled on stone stella and erected in accessible places. Furthermore, judges must read to each defendant the king's decrees relevant to his alleged crime before witnesses are called.

The document deserves its widespread, present fame. Apart from the huge interest that it has for legal historians, it demonstrates to the rest of us how sophisticated Mesopotamian society had become by so early a date in history, as well as how primitive it had remained in many fields. Studying it today, we can draw conclusions from its very existence and costly distribution. It shows, for example, that the state invested heavily in the spread of literacy, surely a good thing in itself. Local officials had to be able to read the law in order to administer it, and citizens were given the incentive to learn to read. At the very least, it enabled them to stand up to judges and prosecutors who were always looking for excuses to extract bribes from them.

***

Contemporaneous with Hammurabi's Babylon, but further up Mesopotamia, was one of the most unusual political phenomena that the world has produced, the Assyrians. Their state, which at times became an empire stretching from Cyprus in the Mediterranean to today's southern Pakistan on the Arabian Sea, astounds with its continuity, even if for short periods it had to pay homage to its fellow Semites in Babylon. It lasted from its foundation as an independent city state based on the temples of Assur on the Tigris in around 2025 BC to its traumatic final overcoming in 609 BC. With an endurance of 1416 years, its longevity beats that of the much-later Eastern Roman Empire in Byzantium by almost three centuries and, as everyone knows, states gain wisdom in continuity. Thus by the end of what scholars call the Early Assyrian Period in the fourteenth century BC, Assyrian women had the right to petition for divorce and slaves were often only slaves in name. Most were servants who could terminate their contracts at will. Remarkably, the earliest Assyrian rulers dared not even give themselves royal titles. They were called "governors on behalf of Assur" and may have been elected for a finite duration by a council of elders. Assur was the city's ancestral deity and the notion that a ruler is a servant of the people can be expected to have survived in folk memory long afterwards. We see echoes of it in the public declarations of the later empires. The Assyrians did, unfortunately, acquire infamy for the cruelties they inflicted on their foreign conquests later – elevating terror almost to the status of a religious duty – but we can also see that they developed a sophisticated philosophy of state and sustained a powerful civil society that in effect, if not in law, limited the liberties of the ruler.

A legacy of the Babylonians that touches our lives today all over the world is the seven-day week. Contemporaneous with the Babylonians, other civilisations that had developed independently had their own designations of the number of days in their regular periods of work and rest. For example, the Egyptians had ten days, while the Etruscans had eight. The Romans inherited the Etruscan practice and only much later, at the time of the first Christian emperor Constantine, changed over to seven days. By then, the Babylonian week had been adopted

16

by the Jews and Phoenicians and others and taken even to the western coasts of the Mediterranean Sea.

***

Ancient Egypt, one of the grandest of the independent civilisations of the time, is outside the scope of this consideration, but another local power that sometimes became an empire cannot be ignored. It was Elam, to the east of Mesopotamia, in today's southern Iran and bordering on the Persian Gulf. It seems, from the start, to have been in sporadic contact with the Sumerians and possibly the civilisation of the Indus Valley, largely in the south-east of today's Pakistan. Elam is important in yet another respect. When, as we shall see soon, Aryan cattle herders such as the Medes and the Persians arrived in the region from the north around a millennium BC, they conquered and settled among the Elamites and borrowed heavily from their political, religious and social practices. The conquerors, particularly in the form of the mighty Persian Empire of the Achaemenids, in turn spread some of their Elamite inheritance farther west into the Greek world, as again we shall see.

Who were the Elamites? As with the Etruscans, their remains are prominent in major museums, but as a political state in history they are obscure. For me, personally, the question has been a most intriguing one since my middle childhood, because in my little Kurdish town of Sahneh in western Iran, we often heard rumours that grave robbers dug up wildernesses in the middle of night in search of Elamite artifacts. The modern town of "Eilam", as its native Kurds call it, was only a few hours away in the neighbouring province of Ilam, as the Persians pronounce the name, and the province borders on Iraqi Kurdistan. Did I have Elamite blood in me, I sometimes asked myself. Today the answer must be a definitive yes, but how much? It is immaterial.

Our genetic inheritances are so mixed that most people of any one region in the world must have a notable admixture of physical characteristics inherited from ancient neighbours.

The best-informed anthropological opinion is that the first Elamites, somewhere in the fourth millennium BC, were a people who achieved a measure of notoriety – that is, political agency – in the ancient city of Anshān. That city's remains are today close to the ruins of the ancient Persian capital, Persepolis, and the modern city of Shiraz, but quite a distance from the Elamites' later capital, Shūshā, to the north-west and closer to Sumer. At times the Elamites are referred to in the Greek world as "Suziāna", after the latter city, but the people called themselves "the Hatamti" and developed their first writing system, known as Linear Elamite, on their own. At times, they became the regional superpower and conquered Sumer and even Babylonia, as well as most of today's southern and western Iran. Indeed, the famous stela of Hammurabi that we discussed above was discovered in the ruins of Shūshā. It had been transferred there as war booty and was evidently valued, for it had been carefully preserved and the cost of its transportation all the distance from middle Mesopotamia to Shūshā must have been formidable. No doubt many wheels and many a wooden axle of the oxen-driven carts perished under its weight.

It is tempting to suggest that the Elamites, as possibly also the Sumerians, were related to the peoples of the Indus Valley, despite the fact that experts believe their tongue to have been a so-called "language isolate". We can envisage even in those most ancient epochs, before our ancestors learned to sow seeds in fields and of whom few had had knowledge of who lived twenty miles away, the odd individual or groups of people broke through the wildernesses to reach another world. They must have included desperate fugitives and exiles, even the plain mad. Be that as it may, the Elamites soon adopted the much more powerful Sumerian system of cuneiform writing and adapted it to suit their own tongue.

What cultural influences did the Elamites exert on their neighbours? Do we think any of their contributions have survived to our time? This is more difficult to answer, but take a look at the monumental sculpture of Persepolis and the palaces of Shūshā, as well as of Babylon and Ninevah, and it becomes immediately clear that much was borrowed. Indeed, the signs are that the influence and prestige of Elamite culture and manners must have been widespread among the first Iranians, that is, the Medes and the Persians. This included their theology affecting the later development of Zoroastrianism, even though Zarathustra's faith did manage largely to retain its original distinction by preserving some of Zarathustra's hymns and core dogmas. One implied example is that Darius felt he had to inscribe his famous proclamation on the rock of Behistun in Elamite, as well as in Old Persian and Babylonian. This may well have been due to few Iranians at the time understanding archaic Old Persian and the site is, after all, situated at the heart of Media. Nevertheless, for this alone, we must be grateful to the Elamites, beside the Babylonians. Darius's resorting to three languages helped archaeologists in modern times to revive the lost art of reading cuneiform scripts. I shall look a little more closely at the intimate embrace that developed later between the conquered Elamites and their conquerors when I come to the rise of Cyrus the Great.

A comment may be added here regarding religion among Mesopotamians, for their creeds, too, would influence subsequent religions and philosophies in the Middle East and beyond, including among the Greeks. Fortunately we have an immense amount of recorded information on what the Mesopotamians believed, even on how their beliefs evolved, for their temples were wealthy institutions and trained large

19

numbers of scribes to commit their beliefs and literature to writing.

One's first impression of Mesopotamian religion – for it was basically the religion of old Sumer – is that it abounded with threatened future punishments and present forebodings. Unlike newly-arrived Zoroastrianism, which took delight in nature and held aloft the hope of redemption if we were – more or less – good, Mesopotamian religion was obsessed with death and suffering in the underworld. One might say it was designed – in the vested interests of the temple and its hordes of priests - to fill the heart of the citizen with fear of what might yet come. We descended into the netherworld when we died, and there, we could eat only dust and live in permanent darkness. Only demigods and demons had some privileges there. Some even sat on golden thrones and had servants and entertainers. In the upper world, satanic forces permeated every minute of one's every day and night, with the ever-watchful eyes of the gods and demons observing our thoughts and actions. Thus were citizens required by the priests to offer food and goods to the temples regularly, so that they, the priests, would beseech the statues of the gods in their temples on our behalfs. We have, for example, the case of one man who makes offerings to the gods to make his penis "as hard as a harp string" once more. The priests must have raised their glasses to themselves every time they prayed for his penis. There were, in addition, religious practices that must have constantly reminded the believer of the imminence of death. For example, corpses were buried in the family house and a clay pipe was connected to their mouth to satiate their thirst. Dead infants were buried near the hearth in the living room, though the latter practice might have brought a little comfort to the grieving mother.

Why was religion in Mesopotamia so overpoweringly superstitious? Some superstition was, of course, inevitable and weighed on all other societies. But contemporary Zoroastrians, still rooted in the well-meaning spirits of their ancestral nomads in the steppes, suffered from the affliction much less. I shall examine the birth and development of Zoroastrianism in more detail in later chapters.

***

While Mesopotamia's initially isolated, agricultural market towns were establishing themselves on the path of becoming the Mesopotamia of record, while they were honing their new writing systems and enhancing their civil and political administrations, an equally important development was brewing in the region to the north-east of the Mediterranean, in that arc of fertile steppe lands that stretches from the river valleys of today's Ukraine towards the top of the Black and Caspian seas. It proved a phenomenon on a world scale. It would result ultimately in the domination of the whole of the world by the peoples who lived there or those who inherited one of their dialects to become known, today, as the Indo-European-speaking peoples, over 450 nations and large, language-communities. The so-called Proto-Indo-Europeans are thought to have been a single people around 6000 years ago. They were cattle herders and fishermen, but they had energy and ambition. They succeeded in bringing to fruition two of the most far-reaching innovations in history. They domesticated the horse and invented the spoked wheel. Until then, wheels were made of solid chunks of wood, cut from trunks of trees and pulled forth by teams of oxen or asses. Now, the domestication of the horse enabled people to manage larger herds of cattle more swiftly while the spoked wheel resulted in the development of war chariots drawn by horses to give their owners an overpowering advantage in imposing their will on their neighbours and rivals, and, once started, the process would not stop. A wealth of archaeological evidence ranging from pottery and grave goods

21

to mummified corpses with red or blond hair tells us that, within only half a millennium or so, the so-named "Pontic-Caspian" peoples reached the Irish Sea in the west and north-western China in the east.

When did these "ancient Ukrainians" – if I may be allowed to call them – reach our area of interest and how did they affect the region? It is a long story, but three groups, the Hittites in Anatolia and the Medes and Persians on the Iranian Plateau need to be examined, for their impact was immediate and immense. The latter two, we are told by Greek sources, spoke dialects of the same language. They could understand one another without any difficulty, implying that they had forked into two branches fairly recently. A fourth branch, the so-called Indo-Aryans of northern India, are also of interest, for their language, Vedic Sanskrit, is close to Avestan, the liturgical language of the Medes and the Persians, and continues, to this day, to help experts interpret the finer points of the psalms, doctrines and culture of the earliest Zoroastrians.

The Hittites were the first group of the new migrants or conquerors to stamp their mark on the region. By around 1700 BC, they had crossed the Bosphorus and seized a vast chunk of Anatolia to reach upper Mesopotamia in the east. They proved eager learners. They adopted the cuneiform script of the Assyrians to their south and came into contact – and conflict – with the Pharos of Egypt. Three-hundred years later, they were a mighty empire who left behind them thousands of records on baked clay tablets.

The Medes and the Persians seem to have gone largely above the Caspian Sea into central Asia and perhaps even through today's Afghanistan before turning west onto the Iranian plateau. Both called themselves "of the Āryā race" and imposed their name on the lands they conquered. They called it Erān Shahr[2].

Perhaps more important than their energy and prowess in war, the Iranian newcomers brought into the region a religion that answered all their basic needs, but was also inspiring enough and elaborate enough to withstand the attractions of the longer-established native creeds and preserve its identity despite borrowing from them. Zoroastrianism is probably the longest-surviving religion in the world. What might explain its success over so many millennia?

Our knowledge remains somewhat insecure on the cosmogony that the newcomers brought into the region with them and the reforms that a prophet among them by the name of Zarath-Oshtra Spitāma – literally meaning "Yellow-Camel-Rich" of the Spitāma clan – instituted in that cosmogony. But scholarship on the subject is growing apace in our time, thanks to the latest works of linguists and archaeologists to enable us to grow more certain on dates and places.

The latest majority verdict suggests that Zarathustra was born somewhere between 1700 BC and 1200 BC, in a place he himself calls Airiianəm Vaējah, likely meaning "the Valley of the Aryan Rapids". No nearby town or identifiable natural phenomenon is mentioned, unfortunately, with the exception perhaps of the Oxus river in central Asia. He refers to it as "the Good River". Scholars have put other clues together to think that the place resembles the mountains of eastern Bactria, in the

---

[2] Erān was pronounced probably as the Kurds still pronounce it, as in the English word "era", and Shahr did not at that time mean city, as it has done in recent centuries. Perhaps an echo of its original Proto-Indo-European origin may be sought in the English word "shire" for a region.

23

Pamirs, north of the Hindu Kush. Zarathustra himself says of Airiianǝm Vaējah that its winters lasted ten months, no doubt indulging in poetic licence (See Franz Grenet in the Wiley Blackwell Companion to Zoroastrianism, 2015). It is also believed that the language he uses for his hymns, later called the Avestan language, was not his mother tongue, but the already near-archaic liturgic language of a place to which he had fled persecution by his fellow Magi. Some scholars have concluded that his father had been a Mede in western Iran while his mother was a native of Central Asia. As for the religion into which he was born – again in central Asia – it was still the polytheistic creed of the Proto-Indo-Europeans similar to those we find still in India's Vedic texts. While Avestan is only very distantly related to Old Persian, the language of Cyrus and Darius, it has much in common with the oldest known Aryan language of India, Sanskrit, suggesting that he lived after the separation of the two peoples, the Iranian Aryans and the Indian Aryans. By how long did Zarathustra trail the separation, we do not know, but it cannot have been too many centuries. From the fact that no cities are mentioned in his hymns, we may conclude that his people had only recently emerged from a long migration as nomadic herders of cattle and sheep to settle down as farmers. One of his main pleas to his God, Ahora Mazdā – "the All-knowing Lord" – is for help against marauding tribesmen who raid the farmers for their cattle and grain.

Zarathustra seems to have been a radical reformer. He proclaimed Ahora Mazdā, "Lord Omniscient", previously only one of a trinity of the most prominent gods of his people, as the supreme power, the only true God and the creator of the good world, who was himself uncreated. Zarathustra angered his fellow Magi by classifying Mithra, the god of the covenant and of fire, as a subordinate deity, as he did also the third previously front-ranking god, Varuna, the lord of the oath and of the rivers and lakes. Ahora Mazda, had seven archangels to assist him in his work of creation. They were called Amesha Spenta, Immortal Holies, who could be described as abstract aspects of himself. They are also personified. All other gods, who were the creatures of his enemy, Ahriman, the creator of whatever was bad in the world, he classified as demons, "the daeva", and each of these has its opposite in the good heptad. Their preoccupation was to spread injustice, suffering and disease on Earth. This version of the divinities, he said, he had received one day in a revelation from Ahora Mazdā himself when he, Zarathustra, was thirty years old, after he had just performed a purifying ablution in a river. When he divulged his revelation, he was persecuted and forced to flee his homeland to seek safety at the door of a neighbouring king. There, he was lucky. King Vishtaspa received him well and accepted the truth of his divine mission. He refers to Vishtaspa as the saviour of the good, for not only did he accept the truth, he also began to champion farmers and the settled people against the thieving nomads. No trace of a Vishtaspa has been found in any of the earliest sources, such as the Vedas in India, suggesting again that Zarathustra had his vision after the separation of the Aryans into their several branches.

Until recently, no trace of Zoroastrian-style fire alters had been found in Central Asia. But these are now being unearthed, showing a trail of pre-Median migrants treading their way southwards and eastwards. Certainly, by the time the Medes and the Persians arrived in north-western and southern Iran, respectively, perhaps around a 1000 years BC, at least their ruling houses seem to have been worshipers of Ahora Mazdā. The Medes seem to have still had some temples that were directed by non-Zarathustrian magi.

Zarathustra has been described as the first philosopher and the first theologian, as we shall see in a moment. To these descriptions we may add "the first self-proclaimed Friend of the Earth", for he abhorred all man-made pollution of the natural environment. His general outlook is optimistic. Ahora Mazdā loves his creation and offers us hope that if we follow his wishes by avoiding hurtful acts against one another and the natural world, we will be rewarded with eternal bliss living beside him and his chosen angels in Heaven. We do not have to lead perfectly good lives. When we die, three angels meet us on the Bridge of Separation and weigh our good acts against our bad ones. If the scale tends towards the good, we will be allowed into Paradise, otherwise Hell. If our record is a fine balance, we shall be sent to Purgatory – a neutral place of existence – for the rest of time. In the meantime, in the present world, which is the second state of the Cosmos, a constant battle rages between the forces of Light and Darkness. It will be apparent to the reader that these basic principles of the Abrahamic religions of today first occurred in Zarathustrianism, the mechanism being that, following the release of their leaders from their Babylonian exile by the Persians, the Jews borrowed them from Zoroastrianism and incorporated them into their own religion. Then they passed them on into Christianity and Islam.

Zarathustrian theology reasons that good and evil exist side by side inside us human beings, though the good will triumph, eventually, with our help. A striking first impression of the Gathas, the prophet's 17 groups of recitations, 136 stanzas of about 6000 words, is that Zarathustra addresses God as almost a friend, with the prophet sometimes even admonishing the Creator for not sufficiently rewarding him with cattle and camels for his toils (This touching brotherhood of man and his creator was noticeable in my father's frequent, pre-dawn monologues with God, though without demanding any grant of camels to the Teimourian family. Perhaps this was because camels were unknown in our mountains.)

26

Few other facts can be deduced from Zarathustra's prayers and professions of faith. But we can see that, though written in strict stanzaic form, they seem to have been meant to be recited, not sung. Let me quote here two short excerpts in a free and, no doubt, contestable, translation, to suggest perhaps why the new prophet's simple and direct message appealed to a primitive, newly-agrarian society, with the distant result that, eventually, it would enable its future adherents, the Medes and the Persians, to resist the more profound-sounding convolutions of the older religions of the region into which they would intrude. The first is from the group of recitations called Yasna (Worship) 31:

> At the beginning, O Mazdā, the Omniscient,
> In thy wisdom, in thy free will,
> Thou gave us the living world, awareness, our souls.
> We long for harmony with thee, O' Mazda.
> We will do our part, through good thoughts, good words, good
> deeds.

And the following from Yasna 41, which may have later been tweaked by his disciples, shows the creed's emphasis on the need to safeguard the environment:

> We honour, O Holy Spirits, the springs, the streams that join
> together to make rivers. We praise the high mountains that produce
> the rivers, the lakes, the meadows and the fields. And we praise
> thee, or Lord, Ahora Mazdā, alongside Zarathustra, as the two
> guardians of the world.

But whatever the new creed's innate qualities, the power and wealth that the Achaemenid emperors and their later successors, the Parthians and the Sasanians, bestowed on their Magi helped spread its prestige to every corner of their vast empires. This was certainly the case in their Ionian Greek colonies in Asia Minor. There, Pythagoras and Heraclitus had frequent contacts with

27

Median and Persian officials and Plato is said to have been visited by a Magus in Athens in his later years. In some of his dialogues, such as the Timaeus, Plato speaks of Zoroaster – the Greek pronunciation of Zarathustra – with respect. Among the Romans, Pliny the Elder praised Zoroastrianism as "the most famous and the most useful" creed. The Christian tale of the three magi following a star to Bethlehem to pay homage to the infant Jesus is similarly worth a mention. The tale uses the prestige of Zoroastrianism to claim divinity for Jesus. Elsewhere, the word "magus" developed into "magician".

On Zarathustrianism's direct influence on the core doctrines of Judaism and Christianity, the late Professor Mary Boyce, London University's renowned authority on antiquity, made the following judgement:

> Gradually many of Zoroaster's fundamental doctrines became disseminated throughout the region, from Egypt to the Black Sea: namely that there is a supreme God who is the Creator; that an evil power exists which is opposed to him, and not under his control; that he has emanated many lesser divinities to help combat this power; that he had created this world for a purpose, and that in its present state it will have an end; that this end will be heralded by the coming of a cosmic Saviour who will help bring it about; … and that thereafter the kingdom of God will come upon earth and the righteous will enter into it as into a garden (a Persian word for which is 'paradise'), and be happy there in the presence of God for ever, immortal themselves in body as well as soul. … These doctrines all came to be adopted by the various Jewish schools in the post-Exilic period …

Amazingly, Zarathustra's influence may even be said to be a force in today's secular world. Who can, for example, read the following prayer by him and not be reminded of Nietzsche's best-selling classic *Also Sprach Zarathustra*? The translation, from Yasna 50, is by the late Belgian expert on Zoroastrianism Jacques Duchesne-Guillemin (1910-2012):

> To me, Zarathustra, the prophet and sworn friend of righteousness,
> Lifting my voice with veneration, O Wise One,
> May the creator of the mind's force show, as Good Mind,
> His precepts, that they may be the path of my tongue.

Would it be going too far to agree with Pierre Bayle (1647-1706) when he described Zarathustra as a philosopher, rather than a theologian? I think that it would not be. Apart from the fact that every major school of theology has a specific world view at its core, all the earliest Greek philosophers who are acclaimed routinely as philosophers were similar to him in their pronouncements. They had at the centre of their teachings theories about the material world, as well as recommended codes of behaviour in society. Take Thales, for example. He said that the world was made of only one substance, water. Zarathustra preached that the whole of the Universe was one giant sacrificial fire. Pythagoras thought otherwise. He said that everything was made of numbers. Others put forth yet other explanations, without any of them producing any evidence that could later be confirmed as convincing. In other words, philosophy, "the love of wisdom", began in the classical world as wholly encompassing the material world and always included a pinch of theology. Zarathustra's cosmogony was probably as elaborate as any of its future rivals. He was a system builder – even though we now use that description pejoratively.

***

The Medes were the first to establish a state, initially as a vassal of the Assyrians and suffering for it. The Assyrians had by then elevated cruelty towards subordinates to a philosophy of statehood. As a result, rebellion became inevitable and did not

29

lay too far in the offing. By the middle of the 7th century BC, concentrated on the city of Ecbatana – today's Hamadan, near this writer's home town – they were strong enough to ally themselves with Babylon and, apparently on their own, sacked the Assyrians' capital Nineva in 612 BC. Subsequently they took possession of northern Mesopotamia, together with parts of central Anatolia.

Just over half a century later, in 550 BC, there was yet another momentous event that would shape the future of the region, perhaps the world, for it would pave the way for the eventual tight embrace of the Iranians and the Greeks in the Hellenistic Age. The young king of the Median vassal state of Pārsā, in today's province of Fars in southern Iran, took over the Median state without resistance and inherited its army and civil service intact. Then, using those powerful instruments, he embarked on a long programme of expansion that, within an astonishingly short time, established him as the overlord of Anatolia, Babylonia, Parthia and even parts of the Indus Valley in the east, creating the largest empire that had ever been, the Achaemenid empire of the "the Medes and the Persians". Who was he?

Cyrus II, or Cyrus the Great, as he was later labelled, was lucky in the circumstances of his birth. He was, so says Herodotus, a grandson of the king of the Medes and, according to one tradition, was born in Ecbatana. As "a prince of the blood", he would have been a familiar figure in court circles there during his childhood. We are told that when, towards the end of his reign, his grandfather Astyages became unpopular among his relatives, ministers and military commanders, a conspiracy was hatched in which Cyrus was urged to invade the country. When he arrived, the Median army went over to him. Thus in the manner of William IV of England, who was imported from Holland – he found himself in charge of a functioning and powerful empire from the start. This seems to be implied also in

30

the famous cylinder seal of the last king of Babylon, Nabonidus. Only three years before his overthrow at the hands of Cyrus, Nabonidus names the Medes, not the Persians, as among his three most dangerous enemies, and it is a puzzle, for by then Cyrus, a Persian, had conquered almost the whole of Anatolia, including many of the Greek city states of Ionia. Why did Nabonidus not mention him while he mentioned the king of Egypt? We are told by some modern scholars that until his conquest of Babylon, Cyrus ruled officially as the king of the Medes, as well as of the Persians. In this light, it was the peaceful inheritance of the throne of Media, with its wealth, bureaucracy and army – an army that had overthrown Assyria - that may explain Cyrus's initial rapid rise in the world. In yet another instance, we see the primacy of the Medes in the eyes of Cyrus himself and of his immediate successors as related by the Greeks. Many a Greek writer referred to the empire of Xerxes and Darius simply as "the Medes". The Hebrew bible, too, refers often to the "laws of the Medes and Persians", as if the Medes continued to be the dominant force in the new empire. We have to conclude that they were, and remained so till the Greek conquest.

Cyrus is important from this study's point of view due to his philosophy of governance. The Jews have elevated him to the status of a Messiah, while Babylonian records praise him for respecting their temples and other institutions. Even the Greek colonies of the Aegean labelled him "the Law-Giver". Could this be largely due to his pragmatism in recognising that he lacked the resources to rule over so many distant regions except through the locals themselves? Governing is costly and difficult without the willing cooperation of subjects. But I tend to think that his policy of tolerance owed much to his personal temperament and religious beliefs. Often he behaved better than was expected of a mighty conqueror, conquerors who liked to boast of how they

31

had decimated those who had resisted them. For example, not only did he liberate the 40,000 or so Jewish exiles from their Babylonian captivity – "By the waters of Babylon we sat down and wept" – he also gave them money and a formal escort to return to Jerusalem to rebuild their Temple of Soloman "as it had been before". Nor did he confine such treatment to the Jews. In fact, the long list of his deeds on his cylinder seal does not mention the Jews. His main emphasis there is on emancipating captives from everywhere in Babylonia. In the poetical words of the late scholar of the history and archaeology of ancient Iran Roman Ghirshman, "A new wind blew across the world", with Cyrus, "carrying away the cries of murdered victims, extinguishing the fires of sacked cities and liberating nations from slavery".

Cyrus's next significant successor was one of his sons-in-law – so we are told – who became known as Darius the Great. Darius does not seem to have inherited Cyrus's tolerant temperament, for as depicted in his detailed rock carvings at Behistun,[3] he sought to secure the foundations of his dynasty by resorting to terror. The carvings depict him trampling on the body of a rebel king while admonishing the others before their execution. In one notorious case, he appointed a Median general with a reputation for brutality over some Greek city states that had rebelled against him. We are told by Herodotus that he exiled the whole population of Miletus – a future font of Greek philosophy – to settle them around the estuary of the Tigris on the Persian Gulf, while, in other places, young men he ordered castrated and young women sold into hareems. Subsequent harsh taxation and

---

[3] Originally "Bagastana", probably a Median compound word meaning God's threshold or dwelling. The present village of the name is in the heartland of old Media and incidentally close to this writer's home town of Sahneh on the old Royal Road from Ecbatana to Babylon and Sardis.

destruction by him caused many recaptured Ionian towns and cities not to recover fully for a couple of centuries.

Darius seems to have elevated some Zoroastrian archangels to semi-divine status, though he is careful always to praise Ahora Mazdā as the only creator of the world. Interestingly, he does not mention Zarathustra. This suggests that, by his time, general acceptance of Zarathustra's central part in the reform of the ancestral religion had still not been achieved among all theologians and all the noble families. That consensus had to wait till the reign of Artaxerxes II of the Sasanians in the fourth century AD, as we shall see in a later chapter.

It might be apt here to quote a passage from Darius's trilingual inscription in Behistun, for it sheds some light on his religiosity and world-view, as well as on his philosophical assumptions regarding human nature:

> A great god is Ahora Mazdā who has created this Earth, who has created this sky, who has created Mankind, who has created happiness for Mankind and who has made Darius King, unique among kings, unique among the many lawmakers. I am Darius, the Great King, King of Kings, king of many lands, king of this vast realm, son of Vishtasp the Achaemenian, son of a Persian, Āryā of Āryan race. Says Darius the Great King: By the will of Ahora Mazdā, these are, in addition to the land of the Persians, the countries that are in my possession, which pay me tribute, which obey my commands. ... Oh, whoever will come after me, avoid the Drūzh (the perpetrator of the Lie), by all your power. If you wish to protect your country [from pretenders to the Achaemenian throne], do not appease the liars and those who commit injustice. Turn your sword upon them. ... And blessed are those who will protect this writing and spread it among the people.

"Happiness for Mankind". We may take it that Darius reflected the official teachings of his religion and state when he advocated happiness as a good in itself, and that since happiness as a concept is as abstract a thought as any, it is philosophy by the standard definition. It implies further that the society from which this king sprang had formal gatherings to formulate its understanding of happiness among the masses. The gatherings were not called philosophers. But they were professionals and most probably constituted the upper ranks of the Magi.

Darius was as successful a conqueror as had been Cyrus and captured even Macedonia on the far side of Greece. This was apparently part of his strategy eventually to cut off the Greeks mainland from any possible allies before pouncing on it in strength. Fortunately for the future of philosophy and science, the Greeks inflicted the grievous defeat of Marathon on him and ended his ambitions. This is not to say that he did not have the cooperation of many Greeks. His fleet was partly manned by Ionians and he had numerous Greek advisors, including his famous physician Democedes. The presence of the latter at his court in Persepolis shows how deeply the Achaemenids favoured many aspects of Greek culture, science and thought.

Darius embarked on a huge programme of improving the roads that linked his various principal cities, Ecbatana, Babylon, Susa and Persepolis, to his many satrapies east and west. The provision of fresh horses and riders at every way station ensured that local governors could be in contact with him at hitherto unequalled speed. It is said that his orders were received in Ionia in seven days. This new network of rapid communications had its uses to civil society, also. Streams of collaborators, traders and artisans arrived to spend significant time in Iranian population centres and took back with them exaggerated tales of power, wealth and knowledge. The new familiarity with Greece also set the stage for the most violent clash of the two civilisations after Darius's death. His son Xerxes – "Khshāyār Shā, King of Kings, King of Babylon, Pharaoh of Egypt, King of [many other] Countries" – invaded the mainland of Greece and burnt down the Acropolis, before suffering his father's humiliation in an ignominious retreat.

However, the exchange of ideas and object with the west did not end in the embers of the old Parthenon. Many a Greek philosopher, doctor and engineer from those communities that had accepted Achaemenid rule flocked into the interior of Iran in search of making their fortunes. On their returns, a majority praised their Iranian patrons for their nobility, religion and world view, with the appreciation being reflected in such writings as the oldest extant Greek play, *The Persians*, by Aeschylus, Plato's admiration for the earlier Persian monarchs in his dialogue on laws, Nomoi, or in the memoirs of Xenophon and the histories of Herodotus. (By the way, the world owes a debt of honour to Xerxes for his burning down of Athens, even if it was not meant as a favour on his part. The returning Greeks buried the damaged statues and other artifacts from the Acropolis in ditches below the hill to pave the way for their rebuilding of the Parthenon. These recovered works – some with their original colours preserved due to lack of light underground – now constitute the backbone of the new, magnificent Acropolis Museum in Athens.)

The Achaemenid empire waned and waxed for another 135 years. At times, it seemed as if all was lost. Egypt, Lydia and others broke away; even Media rebelled. Then a combination of luck and gold and the occasional strong ruler regained nearly all. Even Athens became a willing vassal, though this, in the end, spelled disaster. Philip of Macedonia felt affronted and invaded Athens, putting an end to its long-cherished democracy. Then events took a rapid turn for the worst. Eight years later, Philip's youth of a son, Alexander, invaded the empire and inflicted his revenge on the Great Kings. By then, however, the Greeks and the Persians had lived and clashed together for so long that, one feels, many on both sides no-longer regarded the other as aliens.

35

Greek art, realistic, live and dynamic, dwarfed that of the Iranians, which had remained stylistic and monumental, seeking to impress through size. Ghirshman says:

> The Persians who had mastered Ionia were captivated by its art, which, even before the Median wars, had spread to Greece itself. The master sculptors of Ionia had a great reputation in the most distant countries; political events uprooted and scattered these craftsmen, who carried their art far from their native land, and Darius acknowledged in his 'Charter' that he did not despise the teachings of the Greeks he had subjected to his rule.

As we shall see in the next chapter, about the Greek Seleucid rulers of Iran and the Middle East, the embrace was set to become tighter still.

***

To sum up the first 3000 years of this survey, no document has been unearthed to date to show that ancient Mesopotamians and the newcomers, the Medes and the Persians, set up any academic institutions that aimed at analysing abstract ideas in pursuit of truth. Thus, by this definition, there was no "philosophy" produced in the Middle East in those ancient times in recorded history. Nor was there even history, disciplined history, written there, apart from king lists, celebrations of victories over others, lamentations of conquest by foreigners, etc, though these must not be under-valued. But to say so would set the burden of proof too restrictive. The fact is that, as we saw in the Epic of Gilgamesh, as far back as ancient Uruk, the state was fully understood by its citizens to be based on a moral code of conduct that implied an unspoken, though sacred, contract between the ruler and the ruled, even if it did not achieve the physical form of a signed document. We can also see that, in the local codes of law that have survived, such as that of Hammurabi in Babylon, a universal theory of justice was invoked to underpin the authority of the legislator, with the law-giver boasting the support of the gods for his decisions, for "the gods" here read "the temples", the interpreters of the will of the divine. In retrospect, it could not have been otherwise. Even the smallest market town, let alone the city state that expanded to rule a large region, could not function smoothly without, at least, the passive acceptance of the population. This is fully indicated in the evidence that has come to light of the wealth and popularity of the temples, with their politically sizable retinues. Particularly when the central authority felt insecure, the priests and other representatives of civil society, such as local councils of elders, exerted considerable influence over the ruler. They had to be consulted when it came to raising taxes, let alone decreeing conscription to go to war.

In the case of the Sumerians and their successor states, the Babylonians and Assyrians, the importance of the invention of writing and its advancement from rudimentary pictographs to the cuneiform script that could record sophisticated thought cannot be over-stressed. Without writing, which gradually became a full alphabet, by the time of the ancient Persians and Phoenicians and passed onto the Greeks and others, the sudden explosion of philosophy in ancient Greece that has dazzled the world ever since is hard to envisage.

With the arrival in the region of the Medes and the Persians from the north around a thousand years BC, we can detect a step change in Zoroastrianism. The religion that this particular group of Indo-Europeans brought with them, as we have seen, had the domineering figure of Zarathustra Spitāma as its attractive central figure with an outlook on life and the world that was wholly different from that of the death-obsessed Mesopotamians. Zarathustra is a philosophical thinker and his optimistic, decidedly less superstitious teaching, in the hands later of the powerful Achaemenid emperors, achieved such fame inside and outside the region that a student of Plato felt he needed to compare his master to Zarathustra in wisdom to impress his audience, or that the Christians, much later still, invented the story of three Zoroastrian priests following a star all the way to Bethlehem to prove the divinity of the infant Jesus.

A bird's eye view (as well as a Kurd's eye view!) of the Achaemenids may, in my opinion, be expressed as follows: Such became the prestige of the Achaemenid Great Kings in the region that, after them, all their succeeding empires tried to learn from them, and such was their glory as seen by Iranians themselves in folk history, that all the empires that succeeded them invented family trees claim descent from them. Such was the strength of their memory among the populace afterwards that the present long-lived and various Iranian national identities can, with almost certitude, be claimed to be their creation, and, of course, with statecraft and continuity of societies come recorded history, sophisticated entertainment, high-brow literature and art, all the material that is needed by future generations to ponder in order to produce ethics, religion, and, yes, philosophy.

Altogether, then, although no direct evidence has been unearthed to indicate that ancient Middle Easterners established formal academies of abstract thought, the records that remain of their elaborate religions, law and statecraft imply the existence of advanced educational institutions among them over many centuries. Further, their firm strides over three millennia until the Greek conquest in developing writing, mathematics, time-keeping, astronomy and engineering paved the way for the later flourishing of institutions of intellectual enquiry among the pre-Socratic Greeks. This view may well find proof in the decades to come as scholars translate and analyse the tens of thousands of Mesopotamian and Iranian tablets and inscriptions that remain unread in museum basements all over the world. Yet again, it is believed that we have so far unearthed only a fraction of the ancient libraries and records that existed. For the time being, as things stand, I think that we can even be so bold as to say that without those ancient pioneers, civilisation itself might not have advanced as it has by our time.[4]

---

[4] For a more detailed analysis of the literature and other records of ancient Mesopotamia, see *The Sumerians* by the late Professor Samuel Noah Kramer of Chicago University. The book is freely available on-line.

TWO

The Greek Conquest: The Seleucid Empire

Despite Alexander, the Arabs and the Mongols: the Gate of All Nations, Persepolis.

From 330 BC, when Alexander arrived in Persepolis, until the fall of Seleucia-on-Tigris to the Iranian Parthians 189 years later, the Macedonians and their Greek-led armies laid claim to dominance over most of the former Persian Empire. Despite some rebellions that broke the continuity, this is a considerable period in which the conquerors had a considerable chance to Hellenise their new realms. But they failed. They had arrived with powerful tools with which to achieve their aim: superior military prowess and highly motivated officers greedy for vast new wealth; advanced science and engineering; and the Greek alphabet which had by then been enhanced from that of the Phoenicians to become almost perfectly phonetic and simple to learn. These instruments furnished the new rulers with huge advantages. Their reputation in various fields had even preceded their arrival. After all, they were the people who had thwarted mighty Xerxes, and Xerxes's father Darius had chosen a Greek

41

doctor into whose hands to place his own life. The Greeks also brimmed over with an unshakeable belief in themselves and convinced that "the Barbarians" would be only too pleased to receive the benefits of their higher civilisation. What went wrong?

Many writers have put forth their theories as an explanation, and we know of other instances in history where the conquerors succeeded totally in changing the language, religion, culture and national identity of the peoples they had vanquished. Examples of such defeated peoples include the Phoenicians, Syrians and Egyptians, ancient established nations whose heirs today vie against one another to prove that they are the most faithful of Arabs. But every civilisation and every conquest is unique.

Today, with our vast armies of scholars, science and archaeology, we are in a better position to attempt to settle the questions, and the consensus seems to be that, despite their founding of many new Greek towns that tried to replicate life back in Ionia and Greece, the conquerors' main problem was that, from the beginning, they were too few in number to rule their new subjects except through those subjects' own leaders. One modern writer has said that the Greek cities were mere "islands in the sea of Iran", with their inhabitants only infrequently able to protrude outside their forts. But I think that there were other important factors at work, also. The Greeks did not bring along with them a proselytising totalitarian religion, and they faced a people who had a strong creed of their own, as well as a proud national memory. By contrast, a thousand years later, the Arab Muslims did come so armed, and they succeeded, almost.

No-one knew the Greeks' deficit in numbers better than Alexander himself. He forced his generals to follow his own example and marry an Iranian woman, particularly from an influential family. He wanted every one of his new satraps – satrap itself being a Persian word for regional governor – , as well as lower-ranking officials and commanders, to try his utmost to endear himself to the local aristocracy by "becoming family" with them. As we shall see in a moment, his most significant successor, Seleucus I, did so and became so proud of his Persian wife that he named five new cities after her, with the couple's son, Antiochus I, growing up a virtual Iranian.

To my mind, the Greeks faced also a more subtle, unspoken obstacle. Both the Iranians and Mesopotamians regarded themselves as superior to the invaders, despite the latter's obvious possession of daring, intelligence and knowledge. The Mesopotamians who had invented writing and wrought elaborate theologies of their own were daily reminded of their longer histories by the monumental buildings and statues that adorned their cities, while for the Iranians, the glories of the Achaemenid empire were the memory of only yesterday and a matter of family pride for those who had administered the vanquished empire. There was pain, too, the bitterness of recent defeat and loss. Thus both the Iranians and the Mesopotamians tolerated the invaders and dreamt of salvation to come.

The dearth of Greek numbers meant that, everywhere outside the fortified settlements, scribes continued to go about their daily business in Persian and Aramaic, and everywhere their lawyers interpreted the law as they had always done.

Two acts of Alexander in the vanquished former empire of the Achaemenids feature, more than any other, in Iranian text books of history today: His burning down of Persepolis, and his alleged human sacrifice of some 5000 Iranians to placate the gods on behalf of the soul of a dead friend. The first is an established fact, though it is said that he ordered it when he was drunk. The massacre may be an exaggeration, though Alexander's cruelty

43

and vulnerability to superstition are also established facts. What may be said in favour of the boy conqueror, whose father had employed Aristotle to civilise him, is that he admired the political wisdom of the Achaemenids and, himself being a polytheist, did not try to impose Greek religion on his new subject peoples.

Be the latter assertion as it may, the burning down of the many palaces of Persepolis, dispersed over a large area, does not appear to have been the work of a few drunken hours and it was a disaster, for the new upcoming administration, the Iranians and, of course, future historians. For a whole century and a half since the death of Cyrus in 530 BC, every Great King had lavished a fortune on the town to impress foreign envoys and supplicants. This was particularly true of Xerxes. After his costly retreat from Athens, Xerxes is said to have lost the appetite to stray far from his capitals. Instead, he had concentrated his time on enhancing his father's monumental works and adding more to them. Succeeding Great Kings concentrated their efforts on Persepolis and housed there their diplomatic records, their treasury, and some of their most cherished works of art. Thousands of these documents or fragments of documents on clay tablets have indeed been recovered under the charred rubble by archaeologists, but they concern largely the Treasury. Some of the latter reveal rivalries and jealousies between princes and princesses, together with their extravagances and profligacies. Otherwise, the dearth of vast documentation that the Achaemenids are known to have commissioned on their history, as well as, no doubt, their bardic poetry and other literary and theological works, is puzzling. An explanation may lie in the probability that much of that documentation was recorded on perishable material. Certainly by the time of the next Iranian dynasty, the Parthians, Iranian officials were reported by the Chinese to write on parchment (which implies the obvious step of binding the leaves together to form "codices", or books). This was the view of some later classical authors, though others said that the codex was invented by the Romans. We also know that some Achaemenid scribes wrote on papyrus. Thus in either parchment or papyrus, their records would have fed the flames handsomely for the pleasure of the vandals, as surely did the timber of cedar that had been imported from Mount Lebanon for the roofs. Fortunately, though, the Achaemenids left behind some substantial texts inscribed on stone, as I recounted in the previous chapter.

The same dearth of information also afflicts the age that followed, particularly where it concerns the Middle East, for separate reasons. The Seleucids, as we shall see, did not have their hearts in their eastern territories. They were drawn to regions nearer home and treated such far-flung possessions as Babylonia, Media, Persia and Bactria largely as milking cows, sources of revenue, militia and prestige. As a result, we know much more about them in their newer strongholds of Syria and the Levant. Even there, however, the material is written from the point of view of the Greeks and concern mainly political events, battles and successions.

When Alexander died unexpectedly in Babylon in June 323 BC, on his return from India and at the age of only 33, his generals began to quarrel immediately over who would succeed him. Studying their profiles at this distance leads one to the impression that they were all wild warriors. It makes sense. They had been chosen by Alexander to be his constant companions and he was himself probably a psychopath, or least a sufferer from what today we describe as ADS (attention deficit syndrome). He had famously frustrated his teacher Aristotle with his feral behaviour and widely swaying moods. The most senior of the generals, Perdiccas, was a year younger than Alexander and equally intolerant of dissent. All of the men had been

45

promoted by Alexander for their daring in battle, as well as for their ability to entertain him during their daily drinking bouts, and for their not showing any scruples towards the poor people on whose lives they trampled. They killed hard and lived hard, knowing no other life than fighting or travelling, living for the moment and being brutalised even more severely as they survived the next battle and mourned the grizzly deaths of lovers, friends and comrades.

Now the glue, the centre and the terror of their world was plucked away and, inevitably, their pent-up rivalries rose to the surface. They bickered for days over who would command them henceforth and came to an agreement based on a hypothetical outcome. If Alexander's wife Roxana, a daughter of Darius III, who was pregnant, gave birth to a son, the infant would be named Alexander and proclaimed joint king, together with Alexander's older half-brother Arrhidaeus who was mentally retarded. Until then, Perdiccas would act as regent and commander in chief. Not everyone was happy. Perdiccas's chief rival, Ptolemy, agreed only if he would be given the satrapy of rich Egypt and allowed to leave immediately with a substantial army of his own. Perdiccas consented on the condition that he would appoint Ptolemy's deputy to keep an eye on him in Egypt. The arrangement was clearly going to be temporary. But an eruption of rebellions in all directions did not wait for the dust to settle. In Athens, anti-Macedonian sentiment and nostalgia for lost independence broke out on the streets immediately on arrival of the news and Macedonians were forced to flee, including Aristotle, who fled to his mother's village to die there shortly afterwards. Generals everywhere ejected the Iranian wives that Alexander had forced on them, except, at least one famous exception, already mentioned, the young man Seleucus who would one day end up in possession of Iran and the east and be so proud of his Iranian wife that he would name five new cities after her.

In Babylon, the infantry divisions of the army decided that they could not tolerate any further "Persianisation" of the Macedonian monarchy and plotted rebellion. Perdiccas executed their commander, causing great bitterness. Within a couple of years, however, even loyal Seleucus who had sided with him against all the rebellions would betray him. During a failed invasion of Egypt, he helped assassinate Perdiccas before defecting to Ptolemy. The next twenty years or so were similarly drenched in the blood of the former Macedonian comrades in arms. Even Alexander's mother, let alone his young son and retarded brother, would be murdered. The turmoil put a final end to the Argead dynasty.

My focus here must remain on Seleucus and the Middle East, for a long struggle that lay ahead there to settle finally in a short period of peace until Seleucus could declare himself Basileus in Babylon. Until then, that is, 312 BC, Babylonia, Media and Persis remained the battleground of one invading Greek army after another, sometimes up to 80,000 mercenaries "who lived off the land" and ate out of hearth and home the poor peasantry in the countryside and the artisans of the cities. In trying to imagine what normal life might have come to resemble in the region, I envisage the valley of my own upbringing, laying, as it does, east to west on the main road that connected Ecbatana to Babylonia, Syria and Greece. The inhabitants must have spent daylight hours on the floor of the valley and the nights in the hills. They would have been constantly on the watch for clouds of dust caused by soldiers approaching on the horizon, for woe befall them if they kept a grain silo in the valley to sustain them, let alone a daughter who would make an instant sex slave and camp cleaner for the soldiers. The population of the cities would have plummeted to historical lows, and famine, poverty and

47

disease would have been rife. Regional satraps would have been constantly calculating which war lord had a better chance of triumphing over his rivals. Loyalty would have been openly on sale.

In the absence – as far as I can find out – of documentation or archaeological evidence, we cannot be certain to what extent prosperity improved once Seleucus became firmly established in the east. The dying down of large-scale fighting would have certainly been welcome, and the satraps would have had a vested interest in promoting trade and agriculture. But the satraps were often themselves largely autonomous tyrants and fought between themselves. This internal strife deepened when Seleucus transfer his capital from Babylon to a new city that he was founding on the Tigris and named after himself. A large-scale removal of artisans from Babylon and elsewhere to Seleucia-on-Tigris began quickly to hollow out the other cities and especially spelt the end for ancient Babylon. Worse was to follow. His son and successor, Antiochus – though a proud Iranian on his noble-born mother's side – transferred the capital again to yet another new city, Antioch, this time on the distant coast of the Mediterranean. Thence forth, the Seleucids looked on their eastern territories primarily as royal estates to be exploited for gold, grain and militia. Inevitably, this brought in its wake significant political change, as we shall see in the next chapter on the rise of the Iranian Parthians.

Greek settlement was not evenly spread. It was more concentrated on rich and nearby Media, roughly Iran's present central region, its west and north-west. As a result, in many a future struggle against the Iranians, including the Parthians from north-east Iran, the satraps of Media were able to muster enough Greek and mercenary forces in support of the king in Antioch to thwart the insurgents.

The situation in far-flung Bactria was different. There, the Greek colonists felt abandoned by Antioch when they needed help against relentless waves of nomadic invaders from further north and east. Instead, Antioch called on them to send in more soldiers and revenue for its own wars in the west. Thus did the Bactrian Greeks break away and combine in rebellion with their Iranian subjects to found a long-lasting Graeco-Bactrian kingdom that thrived and expanded to the borders of China long after the decimation of the Seleucids by the Romans. Together with their successors, the Indo-Greek and the Kushan empires, they an indelible mark on subsequent social life and religious thought in central Asia and India, including the formation of the so-called Graeco-Buddhist religion.

Curiously, a truer image of the impact of Greek rule over the Middle East emerges into view after the invaders are expelled from the region, when Arshak or Arsaces I of the Parthians captures Seleucia-on-Tigris and crowns himself Shāhānshāh as a successor to the Achaemenids. The struggle took a long time before it reached that stage and had many ebbs and flows. I shall dwell on the subject briefly in the next chapter, on the first resurgence of the Iranians after their subduing by Alexander, but first, a few words would be apt on one of the Seleucids' enormously important, though unintended, contributions to civilisation.

It is called the Seleucid Era, a system of continuous year counting that became the direct predecessor of today's Christian or Common Era. It eased the work of subsequent historians, and it widened immeasurably the mental horizon of the citizen of every land where it was installed. Previously, when every calendar began its Year One with the crowning of the latest ruler, by necessity only the highly educated knew something of their own people's history before it. Now, suddenly, the past gained centuries of events about which reasonably accurate conversation might be conducted, and not only among your own fellow citizens. Time could be said to have been born anew.

Not surprisingly, it was adopted widely. We find it the basis of *The Jewish War* by Flavius Josephus, the Jewish-Roman historian, and we find it surviving even among Jewish lawyers in Yemen in the twentieth century. In between, there are numerous other examples of its popularity. A famous Christian stele in Syriac in the former Chinese imperial capital of Chang'an says that it was erected there in "The Year of the Greeks 1092 (781 AD).

Anno Graecorum in Latin, AG for short, was not the first continuous system of historical progression. The Babylonians had set up one of their own and it seems likely that awareness of it gave Antiochus I, who knew Babylon well and who started the new system, an inkling of its attractions. Nevertheless, it remains a matter of debate why he did institute it. The most convincing explanation for his decision seems to be that he wanted to avoid confusion. He had been joint-king with his father, Seleucus, for twelve years before Seleucus died in 281 BC. After him, his own son, Antiochus II, presumably did not dare to return to the regnal practice for fear of being seen to dishonour the memory of the founder of the dynasty. So the practice became established and it suited everyone, including the monarchs themselves who continued to appoint their heirs as co-rulers with them to reduce the danger of dynastic strife.

Whatever the explanation, and even though complications did arise when the Macedonian court in Antioch chose a date in autumn as the beginning of the new year, while the Babylonians and Iranians were allowed to stick to spring, as had been their practice for a long time, the new calendar eased the work of scribes and chroniclers immeasurably and immediately. It put an end to the incomprehension that was the result of various regnal eras. Having said that, in Iran and elsewhere, including the Graeco-Bactrian Kingdom, unfortunate returns to the old system were attempted and these sometimes create difficulties for historians today, when they try to date specific events.

How did it arise precisely? Seleucus had first declared himself an independent ruler in Babylon on April 3, 312 BC, but he was ousted and driven into exile at the court of Ptolemy in Egypt by his arch rival Antigonus "the One-Eyed". He was, however, able to return in 305 and abided by the old regnal system until his death in 281. At that moment, his son and heir – the half-Bactrian Antiochus – found himself facing a puzzle. Should the new era begin then, when he himself became undisputed king, or twelve years earlier when his father had declared him join monarch? Antiochus chose a third way. He decided that, henceforth, the years would be counted continuously from, not the final declaration of his father's suzerainty over Babylon, but the first, 312. Perhaps we should declare Antiochus as the patron saint of historians.

THREE

The Parthian Empire: Retreat from Hellenism

5

The Parthians were a confederacy of north-east Iranian tribes related to the Persians and the Medes. They rebelled against their Greek rulers in the middle decades of the third century BC and became, around a hundred years later, one of the major empires of the Western world and Rome's most formidable rival and neighbour. They also lasted almost five centuries, making them the longest-lived polity in Iranian history.

---

[5] A remarkably life-like sculpted head of a Parthian prince wearing a Greek-style helmet found in the royal cemetery of Nisa, Turkmenistan, 2nd century BC. It is likely to have been carved by either a Greek sculptor or a Parthian pupil.

53

The Roman historian Justin says of them that their language was "midway between Scythian [to the north and east of the Caspian Sea] and that of the Medes [to the south-west of that great inland lake]. This may well refer to the language of their subjects in the former satrapy of Parthia, rather than that of the initial ruling house, which seems to have been of recent Scythian descent from around the Aral Sea. They captured the vast region of Parthia that today straddles the borders of Iran, Turkmenistan and Afghanistan. The Parthians, the bulk of the population of the new state, shared an origin with the Persians, too, as I suspect may be hinted in the similarity of the names of their two eventual regions of settlement, Pārthāvā and Pārsā. The Persians, who preceded them on their migration through that same region southwards might have easily given their name to the land before they left it to move on further south, their common origin being their Aryan ancestors in the north-western steppe going all the way back to north-eastern Ukraine. As with these other Indo-European invaders, they remained excellent horsemen, giving their name to the "Parthian Shot" in Western languages. This was on account of their cavalry's tactic of feigning defeat to draw the enemy behind them before turning back in the saddle to shoot at their pursuers.

We come across Parthia as a political entity first in Darius's long declaration on the rock of Behistun in the late sixth century BC. He mentions it among the regions that had rebelled against him. Under the Greeks, it became a satrapy but its inhabitants remained deeply aware of their Iranian identity and aspired to the legacy of the Persian Achaemenid Great Kings, as is betrayed in their leaders' claiming descent from them, as well as their attachment to Zoroastrianism. When the Seleucids transferred their capital to the far west in Antioch and their Iranian satrap Andragoras rebelled, a chieftain of the recently-arrived Parni confederation of tribes saw his chance to seize power. It seems to have proven an easy task.

According to one account, Arshak I, the founder of the new dynasty, was himself no Scythian newcomer, but a native Parthian. Whatever the truth, Arshak[6] became a revered figure among his descendants to the extent that Arshak became the eponymous royal name of all future Parthian sovereigns, making rather difficult the work of distinguishing their coins from one another. One of the most successful of the Arshaks was a great grandnephew by the personal name of Mehrdāt (Mithridates) I, a century later. He drove the Greeks out of Media and Mesopotamia and transferred his capital to the banks of the Tigris. His name, which means Mithra-given indicates that the new state revered the old Indo-European god among its chief saints, one of the seven manifestations of the spirit of Ahūra Mazdā in Zoroastrianism.

The Parthian aristocracy practiced polygamy and often married their step-siblings. This, too, had been practiced by some of the Achaemenids. One Parthian monarch, though, exceeded the boundaries of decency to her cost. She was an Italian courtesan and a Roman emperor's gift by the name of Musa. On the death of her royal husband or lover, she married her own son to declare herself co-monarch with him. The legal ruse seems to have backfired, even if it were not a real marriage. A palace rebellion resulted in her execution.

The rise of the Arshakids or Arsacids can, at this distance, be seen as the Iranians' first successful regression from the policy of Hellenization that had been put in place by the Seleucids. This is despite their early kings labelling themselves as "Philhellene"

---

[6] From Old Iranian Arshan, for hero.

on their coinage. Was the latter act merely a political ploy to mollify the many Greek colonies that the Seleucids had left behind them in Iran? It may well have been so and was certainly seen as such. But it may also have been sincere. Arsacid rulers often spoke Greek and valued Greek art and culture, which was clearly of a higher level of attainment. This is well illustrated by the most iconic moment recorded in their history in 53 BC, not because it heralded a great military victory over Rome, but because it indicated a high degree of cultural sophistication on the part of the monarch concerned. We hear that the head of an invading Roman emperor, the Triumvir Crassus, was brought in on a platter to show the monarch, who was visiting his vassal and son-in-law, the king of Armenia. As the two kings were interrupted by the joyful – though gruesome – evidence, they were watching a performance in Greek of the Bacchae by Euripides. Even the choice of the play is significant. A favourite of world theatre to this day, it is a commentary on what happens when religious fanatics take over a country, a lesson that today's Iranians under the ayatollahs continue to learn at their cost.

Unlike the Achaemenid Persians, who had lived alongside the Elamites and neighboured Media, Sumer and Babylon for several hundred years before they rose to claim their own place in the sun under Cyrus, the Parthians were a largely nomadic people, or at least only recently settled. What foreign thoughts, manners and practices they had absorbed were largely from their former Greek rulers and their new Greek subjects, the Hellenic colonists. After they established their new kingdom, they also maintained a close relationship with the Graeco-Bactrian empire on their eastern border.

The Arshakid monarchs made a point of giving their heirs resounding Iranian personal names – Tīrdāt, Farhād, Khosro, Orod, Ardavān – and claimed descent from one of the most illustrious of the Achaemenids, Artakhshīr (Artaxerxes) II. This

56

is generally dismissed as a feign to claim legitimacy for their original rebellion, but it carries an important message. It is a proof that the memory of the first great Iranian empire of the region had driven deep roots among its subjects, and that any new state was expected to honour the ways of its Persian predecessor. We may also assume that Achaemenid princely families who had been appointed to high office under the Seleucids continued to wield influence, both cultural and religious.

Nevertheless, as already mentioned, their most recent cultural influencers remained Greek. For almost a hundred years, Seleucid officials and settlers had been encouraged formally to intermarry and intermingle with locals to consolidate their grip on the region. This is most evident in Parthian art, architecture and inscriptions. It took the new state a century or two into its expansion in the south and west to gain enough confidence in itself to flaunt fully its Iranian identity. It was only then that the recession from the Hellenist world became formally acknowledged.

To what extent were the Parthians Zoroastrian in religion? I shall have more to say on this subject when I sum up this chapter, but this is perhaps a spurious question. Religion is often only an informal profession of one's cast or ethnic identity, rather than a deep knowledge of doctrine. If a person says he adheres to a particular faith or attends the gatherings of a particular faith or sect, his claim is accepted immediately at face value, for most adherents of most religions are unable to articulate the core dogmas of their avowed faith. But, be this as it may, we probably owe at least the partial survival of Zarathustra's hymns and attributed sayings in the Avesta to the Parthians. We are told that one of their monarchs, Balāsh I, ordered his scholars to seek out the purported hymns and beliefs of the prophet in their scattered state in order to separate the authentic from the corrupt. Due to the scarcity of source material, however, we do not know if the task was accomplished fully. We must therefore believe only that when the Parthian empire was eventually replaced by the Sasanian, the efforts of the latter in codifying Zoroastrian scripture and practice were better informed to start with. The following legends from the reverse side of many a Parthian coin may be of interest:

> "[This is] Of Arshak, king of kings, the divine manifest, benefactor, just and philhellenic", or "[This is] Of Arshak, great king, son of a deified father, benefactor, the divine manifest and philhellenic.

Note that the monarch did not use their personal names on their coins, but their generic throne name that went back to Arshak, the founder of their dynasty. As a result, we have to rely on their portraits to distinguish one coin from another. Thus when the coins have suffered from over-use, scholars have difficulty dating them.

Parthian rulers were not, by the standards of their own time, including their neighbours the Romans, a vicious sequence. Nowhere have I come across any allegations of atrocities committed by them against civilians, nor the maiming or torturing of rivals and captives. This may well be due to a dearth of records, but might also be explained by the Parthians retaining their recent tribal codes of conduct. Their myriad, lower-level ruling families lived among their subjects and alongside their neighbours and the state was essentially a coalition of a smaller number of the leading families. As for their vasal states, such as Babylonia or the Greek city states inside their borders, they were largely left to their own traditions. Compare this to the behaviour of one Roman emperor who arrived in their capital Ctesiphon to wed a daughter of Ardavān V. Caracalla, who had previously been appeased with large sums in gold not to invade, brought a sizable army with him. Once the entertainment started, he unleashed his soldiers on his unfortunate hosts and murdered large numbers of them before sacking the city. Ardavān managed to escape alive, but he was severely weakened and ended up as the last of his line.

What kind of a society did the Parthians leave behind? It seems as if that same relaxed attitude to difference had brought about a polity that was a fermenting vestibule for ideas. It allowed even for large associations to form to challenge the official religion of the state. One major example is the rise of Manicheism in Ctesiphon, the capital. A brief description of the new religion may illustrate the point.

Manicheism, one of the most philosophical of all religions which would eventually spread to China in the east and Rome and Carthage in the west, arose in the year 248. A precocious boy of 12 years by the name of Māni claimed that he was not of his bodily father, but of divine fertilisation, and that he had been chosen by God as the seal of the prophets. He would complete the missions of Jesus, Zarathustra and the Buddha, among others. The son of a Parthian father from Ecbatana in Media and of a Christianised Jewish mother from Mesopotamia, the boy spoke of his elevation to Heaven for his formal appointment to put together a creed that contained the best of all the current religions of the world. He also had a twin spirit who spoke to him constantly and guided him. Large crowds were attracted, no doubt to the consternation of the Magi at the Parthian court and elsewhere. In his middle twenties, he set off for "India" – apparently with the consent of the Great King himself, by then a Sasanian – to study Buddhism, but in fact proceeded no farther than northern Afghanistan. While there, he feasted his followers in a large cave before telling them that he would be away for a year in Heaven. When his supporters turned up in the same cave a year later, he reappeared to them with a number of paintings that he said he had created in the celestial sphere.

59

On his return to Ctesiphon, a debate or interview is said to have been arranged for the new prophet at court and though he failed to persuade the monarch to the truth of his mission, he was allowed to continue his preaching. Mani was again tolerated by two succeeding kings, until his luck ran out. Wahrām I saw him as a threat to Zoroastrianism or to the state and, sometime between March 274 and February 277, ordered him to be incarcerated. He died shortly afterwards. His followers claimed that he had been martyred for his faith, but other reports say that he was not maltreated. He died surrounded by secretaries and servants.

What were Mani's cosmogony and ethics that made him so attractive to large numbers of people in Ctesiphon, Babylon, and elsewhere? More than his skilful paintings and disappearing tricks, he preached that he had been chosen by God to reveal the inner, hidden truth of religion, and he borrowed essential elements from all the main religions of the region to dispel any impression that he intended a revolution in belief. To this day, echoes of his particular variety of esoteric Gnostic dualism are clearly detectable among the Druzes and the Yazidis of the Middle East. The hidden truth could not be revealed to the uninitiated. Only after commitment to the new church would the ordinary person be entrusted with it and understand it.[7] He inspired deep devotion among his followers. But that part of the

---

[7] Other echoes of Manicheism can be found in many sūrahs in the Koran, as well as in purported Hadith. One example is the allowing of "taqiyah" or dissimulation which is especially encouraged in Shiism (Koran 16:106). It allows the believer to renounce his faith and even denounce the prophet under threat, for instance in a hostile society, if he feels that his lying would safeguard his survival and therefore the longer-term interests of Islam. Manicheism commended the ploy.

story belongs to a later time and I shall return to it in the next chapter.

For the moment, we might pass one final, overall, judgement on the society that the Parthians had created and handed over to their successors, the Sasanians. Starting from a distinctly tribal, relatively underdeveloped, society, five centuries earlier, Parthian monarchs ended up as sophisticated, Greek-speaking rulers shaped by a long family history of world-class events from which they were urged by their tutors to lean lessons in statecraft. One of these emphasised the importance of equanimity between the various elements of their empire, such as Parthians, Babylonians, Medes, Persians and Greeks, every one of which had its own particular religion or sect or philosophy of society and state. They accepted that they had to rule by proxy, as heads of a larger family of ruling families far and wide. At home, they did not, apparently, succeed in gathering and editing the writings of Zarathustra into one, final, accepted version. But they made a good beginning and certainly handed over to their successors much documentation on Zarathustra that would serve them, the Sasanians, well.

FOUR

The Sasanians: Zarathustra versus Jesus

Philosopher king: Khosro I, "Shāhānshāhi Erān ud an-Erān", d. 579 AD[8]

Philosophy is superior to religion, for religion is always accompanied by doubt, whereas philosophy is the intellectual acceptance of explained ideas. – Khosro I

Chosroes was a prudent and wise man and devoted his life to the assiduous studying of philosophical works ... He took pains to collect the religious books of all creeds and studied

---

[8] "King of Kings of Iran and non-Iran". An ornamental plate depicting Khosro I, Anūshak Rawān "Immortal Soul", known widely in Iran and elsewhere in the Middle East today as Anowshīrvān the Just. Bibliothèque Nationale de France, Paris.

them that he might learn which one was best and most truthful.
– John of Ephesus (d. 588AD).[9]

His mind he filled with the doctrines of Plato. – Paul the
Persian[10]

Proving perhaps that nations often harbour long memories of
their past, the Iranians in the first quarter of the third century AD
produced yet another long-lived empire that harked back to
Xerxes and Darius and vied over with Rome for the title of the
strongest in the world. This is how a modern scholar – one who
specialises in the history of Rome – updates our view of the
Sasanians as compared with the Romans and Byzantine:

> Sasanian studies have progressed rapidly in the twenty-first
> century. While the state was widely seen as rather a
> disorganised and disunited feudal one even in the recent past,
> our latest evidence points to a highly organised and successful
> empire whose intensified irrigation, increased food production,
> unprecedented population growth in places, flourishing urban
> culture and large-scale military infrastructure rivalled and in
> some respects surpassed those of the western world in late
> antiquity.[11]

There is much of interest to say of a long-lived empire whose
deeds and decisions continue to reverberate in our lives today,

---

[9] John of Ephesus was a bishop of the Miaphysite Syriac Orthodox
Church who died in prison in Constantinople. In his History of the
Lives of Saints, he apologises for having to praise "a Magian
enemy", i. e. Khosro.

[10] Khosro's principal teacher of philosophy, a Nestorian bishop
who converted to Zoroastrianism in later life and wrote at least one
treatise on the philosophy of Aristotle for the king.

[11] Professor Eberhard Sauer in *Sasanian Persia: Between Rome
and the Steppes of Eurasia.* Edinburgh University Press, 2017.

thirteen-and-a-half centuries after its demise. But that belongs to a historical enquiry and fortunately many books have been devoted to it recently. I shall, instead, proffer here a personal opinion on its overall impact on late antiquity and draw the briefest possible portrait I can of the dynasty at its centre in the shape of a couple of its most consequential emperors or *shāhānshāh*s, before examining its philosophical and theological underpinnings and aspirations.

A primary fact that explains much about the Sasanians is their being a continuation – in a social and even a political sense – of the Parthians they had overthrown, though they would themselves have denied it. With the exception of a few over-powerful emperors who were able to impose their will on the paramount noblemen of the previous regime, most Sasanian rulers settled for persuasion, rather than coercion, in their dealings with what centres of patronage remained of the Parthians. This had deep implications for Sasanian politics, art, lifestyle, religion and foreign relations. Through the centuries of the Parthians' intimate association with the many Greek colonies that the Seleucids had left behind in Iran, and through the widespread use of the Greek language in diplomacy and bureaucracy, the Sasanians were affected by, and imitated, the policies and traditions of both the Arsacids and the Seleucids. This meant that the new empire was, for much of its time, a confederation of rulers, rather than the tyranny of an emperor over obedient vassals. The emperor at the centre was recognised as the titular head of the empire and received tribute and military aid in emergencies from his subordinate shahs, but it was understood that he – in one two cases she – would not interfere in their internal, hereditary affairs. The arrangement made sense. The King of Kings was saved the need to maintain expensive standing armies in the north and east, the Parthian heartland. In time the two blocks converged culturally and formed strong

65

emotional bonds through dynastic marriages, and both emphasized their upholding of the Zoroastrian faith as their inherited creed, though they often disagreed on interpretations of the faith's doctrines and traditions, and both were sentimental in their attachment to the concept of Erān Shahr, their original Aryan homeland of legend. The resultant stability enabled the new empire to flourish militarily, economically and culturally, in time its influence reaching as far east as China. It is generally believed now that an eventual resurfacing of old clashes of interest between the Sasanian imperial family and its Parthian partners, exacerbated by its ruinous wars with the Byzantines and a widespread popular disgust with the excesses of its Zoroastrian priesthood, was one of the main causes of its collapse at the hands of Muslim tribes out of the Arabian desert.[12]

A major achievement of the Sasanians was their revival of Persian as the lingua franca of the vast region over which they came to preside. It seems that a nucleus of Pahlavi or Middle Persian – whose simpler grammar made it easter to master than Old Persian – had already come into being in the latter days of the Achaemenids. Under the Sasanians, through both patronage and seepage, the newer tongue spread rapidly and was enriched through borrowings from Parthan, a related Iranian language, as well as Aramaic and Greek. Later still under the Sasanians – as illustrated by a short quote I shall make in a moment from the *Books of the Deeds of Ardashīr the Pāpagian*[13], today's Farsi or New Persian came into being and spread even farther.

---

[12] See *Decline and Fall of the Sasanian Empire: The Sasanian-Parthian confederacy and the Arab conquest of Iran* by Parvaneh Pourshariati. I. B. Tauris, London, 2008.

[13] Kārnāmagi Artakhshīri Pāpagān.

The Sasanians began in a rebellion in the present-day province of Fārs, old Pārsā, in southern Iran, at a time when the Arsacids had been weakened by endless wars in the west against Rome, civil wars among themselves and intrusions by marauding Hunnish and Scythian tribes in the north-east, made worse by the first appearance of a new pestilence from the east, smallpox.

The Sasanians' founder Sāsān appears not to have known the names of his ancestors beyond a couple of generations, suggesting that he rose from a humble background. We find corroboration for this assertion in a proclamation by the last Arsacid emperor, Ardawān IV, against Sāsān's son Ardashīr I, as someone who had "been brought up in the tents of the Kurds" and not entitled "to aspire to the glorious throne of the ancients". This, of course, did not stop the challenger from inventing a family tree for himself to link him to Darius III, the last of the Achaemenid Great Kings. A later Sasanian text, however, gives the game away, even though it tries to combine both accounts. Accordingly, despite his ancient royal blood, Ardashīr's father Sāsān had fallen on hard ground and earned his livelihood as a shepherd in the service of a local governor called Pāpag. It makes some primary historical errors about the Greeks and the Romans, but remains informative. It also has literary charm for today's Persian speakers due to its partially archaic lexicon. It shows that today's New Persian or Farsi was almost fully formed in the six century. The text is called *The Book of the Deeds of Artakhshīri Pāpagān*:

pad kārnāmagi ardakhshīr ī pābagān idūn nibisht istād kū pas az margi alaksandari rōmāyīg ērān shahr rāi 240 kadag-khwadāi būd. spahān ud pārs ud kustīhāi awish nazdīktar pad dasti ardawān sālār būd. pābag marzobān ud shahryāri pārs būd ud az gumārdagāni ardawān būd ud pad stakhr nishast. pābag rāi īch frazandi nām-bordār nebūd ud sāsān shubāni pābag būd ud hamwār abāg gūspandān būd ud az tōhmagi dārā ye dārāyān būd ud andar duzh khwadāyīhi alaksandar ū wireig ud nihān-rawishnīh īstād ud abāg kordān shubānān raft.

In the Book of the Deeds of Artakhshīr the Pāpagian has been written thus: After the death of Alexander the Roman, Iran was divided into 124 principalities. Ispahān and Pārs and their near districts were in the hands of King Ardawān and he had appointed Pāpag to be his marzbān (military governor) and shahryār (subordinate king) in Pārs with his seat in [the city of] Stakhr. Pāpag had no name-carrying children (sons) of his own. Sāsān was his shepherd and was constantly with the sheep. [But] Sāsān was of the seed of Dārā of the Dārās [Darius III]. During the misrule of Alexander, Sāsān rebelled and [at times] went into hiding. He went [to live] with Kurdish shepherds.

Some scholars (the latest being Touraj Daryaee) interpret the designation Pāpagiān to mean that Ardashīr was a son of Pāpag the governor. I see no ground for this deduction as "Artakhshīri Pāpgan" can mean merely to pertain to the house of Pāpag". The text just quoted states clearly that Pāpag had no children of his own "to carry forth his name". The implication must be that Pāpag either adopted Sāsān as a son, or else gave him a daughter in marriage and bestowed his name and position on him.[14] The document has other implications, too. One is that Sāsān was a Kurd, for he was so indistinguishable from the Kurds that he could hide among them for long periods. The suggestion in turn strengthens King Ardawān's accusation against Sāsān's son and

---

[14] The tradition has survived into modern times. For example, the strict pronunciation of my own name in Persian is: "Hazhīre Teimouriān", while it is "Hazhīri Teimouriān" in Kurdish, whose sounds and lexicon seem closer to Middle Persian than is today's Persian. But I am no descendant of a Teimour. Only a great grandfather of mine adopted the name of his spiritual mentor Teimour of Bānyāran as his surname. This was after Teimour had been executed for blasphemy in the early 1900s.

successor, Ardashīr, for if the family were not Kurds, the King's accusation would lack resonance among the public and paint him as a liar.[15]

Be that as it may, more documents have survived of the events that followed. It took a decade or so after a number of military setbacks before the former shepherd and his two sons, including his successor Ardashīr, defeated and slayed Ardawān in 224 AD and subdued all other challengers to their ascent within the former Arsacid empire. Ardashīr also expelled the Romans from Mesopotamia and the Caucasus.

His triumphs were followed by the achievements of his son Shāpūr I, when he defeated and imprisoned the Roman emperor Valerian – a cruel persecutor of Christians – in 260, in the process exacerbating the civil unrest in Europe that contributed to the eventual division of the Roman empire into two wings, east and west. Thence onwards, the Sasanians became the nemesis of eastern Romans and at times reached even Egypt. In between bouts of fighting, there were also much cultural exchange and not a few dynastic marriages between the two great powers.

The new dynasty appears to have acquired philosophical aspirations early. Another text that purports to hark back to the

---

[15] The question is of a sentimental nature to my fellow Kurds who strongly identify with the Sasanians and, before them, the Medes. The Sasanians would in time shift the centre of their gravity to western Iran, old Media, before designating the former Seleucid city of Ctesiphon on the Tigris, with its large Kurdish population, their winter capital. In 1973, as a journalist, I spent a couple of weeks in a Kurdish village in Iraqi Kurdistan near the border with Syria. I was struck by the number of people, young and old, who bore Sasanian names.

reign of the second Sasanian Great King, Shāpūr I, relates how the government set up a mission to collect the best thinking of the age regarding secular matters. The results were then sent to the royal treasury for safe keeping. The list given of the subjects is startling in its range and comprises almost all topics that had earlier preoccupied the philosophers of Greece. They include: "movement, time, space, substance, chance, becoming, decay, transformation, logic and other crafts and skills that were dispersed in India, Rome and other lands".[16]

However, such is the shortage of surviving documents from the era on this subject that we must turn to a much later Great King to put a face to the development of philosophy among the Sasanians. He is Khosro I in the sixth century, known today by his posthumous epithets *The Just* and *The Immortal Soul*. He ruled for 48 years and was, for much of that long reign, secure on his throne. He was thus able to indulge his curiosity at vast expense. As a result, as we saw at the start of this chapter in that quote from his Byzantine contemporary, John of Ephesus, he perhaps deserves the fame that he gained in posterity and that we are justified if we call him philosopher king.[17] He made his state the predominant centre of learning in the West – with three major universities and the first hospitals in the world – and he encouraged the settling in his major cities of teachers from both Byzantium and India. These included many leading Miaphysite and Monophysite (Nestorian) priests who had come to be

---

[16] Daryaee, p83.

[17] In my century-old, heirloom copy of the *Shāhnāmeh,* with its huge dimensions of 11 by 15 inches (29 by 44cm), I count that Ferdowsi devoted 4,548 verses to his life and deeds, perpetuating his legend throughout the Persianate world from Istanbul to Khujand as the model of a wise and just ruler.

persecuted as heretics by their fellow Christians in Constantinople. Most famously, he welcomed the Neo-Platonist philosophers of the Academy in Athens when they were expelled by Justinian I in 529, though his tolerance did not extend to either Catholics – whom he suspected as possible Byzantine agents – or Iranian Manichaeans whom he saw as a threat to the Zoroastrian church, though he was himself probably a convinced sceptic. Politically, Khosro achieved stability over several decades by deterring the Romans from further pestering his possessions in Mesopotamia, Armenia and Georgia, while also containing Turkic and Sythian incursions in the north-east. Such was his sense of security that he allowed Jews, Buddhists and Eastern Orthodox Christians to roam freely over the empire.

Khosro has left us a brief autobiography, which unfortunately exists only in an Arabic translation of uncertain integrity.[18]

Despite his fame for justice, Khosro could be extremely ruthless. He is said to have executed some of his brothers and many of his relatives after they had rebelled or plotted against him. Thus must we interpret his renowned justice as not necessarily emanating out of genuinely-felt altruism, but political necessity. In parallel with a later king in the far west, Henry II of England some six centuries after him, Khosro's prime motivation in setting up a new network of judges and inspectors may well have been to break up the power of the great land-owning families. He distributed their lands among smaller landowners who would

---

[18] *Sirati Anushīrwān*, in the eleventh-century Neo-Platonist philosopher Ibn Meskawaih's *Tajāreb al Umam (The Experiences of Nations)*, as edited by Qāsem Amāmi, Tehran, 1987, pp 100-110. Though Ibn Meskawaih was a Persian and sentimental about his people's past, doubt must remain on the extent to which he, as a Muslim official, dared to be faithful to the original, or whether his text is a summary or the full original.

71

thenceforth be dependent on his patronage. By doing so, he added a new class to society, beside the nobility, the Magi and commoners. The new class became known as the dehgāns – village lords – who acted also as tax collectors and were obliged to provide Khosro's armies with soldiers. The initiative proved of long-lasting importance in cultural and religious terms, too, for in the dark centuries that followed the Arab conquest of Iran, the dehgāns played a pivotal part in preserving Zoroastrianism, Iranian ethnic identities and languages from the conquerors' systematic attempt to annihilate them. This was the fate that befell Syria and Egypt. United by their attachment to Zoroastrianism and the Iranian national memory, the dehgāns resisted the spread of Islam long enough to transfer nuclei of the Zoroastrian priesthood to India – where the migrants became known as the Parsees, the Persians, and also to preserve what remained of Middle Persian history and literature for future generations such as Ferdowsi.

Anushirwān's early reign was unusually turbulent, for he was not his father Kawād's eldest son, though his favourite as a successor. As crown prince, he was given the task of putting down the rebellion of an elder brother before suppressing a larger uprising by other relatives after he ascended the throne. A second challenge rose when a communistic political movement, the Mazdakites, had gained a widespread following after a famine. It was led by two Zoroastrian priests by the names of Zardosht and Mazdak. The movement had acquired such popularity that Anushirwān's father Kawād had felt compelled to embrace it in public and partly to use it to undermine the power of the most powerful of his subordinate shahs. Anushirwān may have been chosen as a successor because, unlike his elder brother, he feared the threat of the Mazdakites. He suppressed them and executed Mazdak. They advocated radical equality in the possession of property and, it is claimed, even wives and children. They toppled many local landowners and disrupted the collection of taxes. After their suppression, Khosro extended and deepened the programme of land and taxation reform that his father had begun, exempting the poor and the old from taxation altogether. Khosro also accepted that the empire was too large for a single standing army under a single commander, the Ērān Spahbad. He set up four separate armies in the north-east, north-west, south-west and south-east.

Before I examine Khosro's philosophical beliefs in a little more detail, it is perhaps worth mentioning that in the popular imagination of the Persianate world today, his name is inextricably linked to two of his advisors, for this has philosophical implications. One is a man by the name of Borzuyeh whom he sent to India to research the wisdom of that vast and ancient civilisation. Borzuyeh brought back with him in about 550AD a number of books and had them translated from Sanskrit into Pahlavi. They included a version of the famous Panchatantra or Five Discourses. This is a complicated, interwoven series of stories mainly by two wise jackals who tell tales to reflect on, and to ridicule, the politics and foibles of humans. Borzuyeh gave the book a new name, Kalilag ud Damnag, after the two jackals, and it has proven a widespread success ever since, particularly after it was translated from Persian into Syriac, Hebrew and Arabic in later centuries. One version that subsequently swept through Europe is called the Fable of Bidpai.

The other sage with whom Khosro is linked in popular memory is the more famous Wuzorg Mehr (Great Mithra), a nobleman and courtier from the Parthian clan of the Karens. Known as Bozorg-Mehr today, he has become the personification of reason and Aristotelian moderation in human affairs. Many anthologies of his writings appear to have circulated after his death and some of these have survived – at least partially – in subsequent Islamic literature in Arabic and Persian. Many legends have been woven around him, too. One is that he invented the board game backgammon in reply to a vassal king in western India who had sent Anushirwān the game of chess. The Indian had afterwards to confess that the Iranians were the wiser and deserved the tribute that he paid them annually. They had realised that intellect – as in chess – was not always the key to human happiness, but that chance, as in backgammon, also played a vital part. At any rate, Wuzorg Mehr has left us the world's first manual of chess.

From our point of view here, however, it is the writings of Khosro's principal teacher of philosophy which throw greater light on his sovereign's beliefs and the philosophical interests of his counsels. The man is known in European literature as Paul the Persian and was a former bishop of the Nestorian Orthodox Church who had aspirations to be appointed archbishop of Persia. On being denied this promotion, it is said, Paul converted to Zoroastrianism. Whatever the truth, two – or perhaps three – of his treatises on philosophy have survived. One is known specifically to have been written in Pahlavi for Khosro and is a commentary on Aristotle's logic. A later Syriac translation of it has survived and can be found at the British Museum, but remains untranslated into modern languages. The other is a general introduction to philosophy and is important for Paul's version of the delineation of the various branches of the discipline.

It seems to have been Paul who convinced Khosro of the superiority of reason over faith. He taught that faith – dependant as it was on the authority of the prophets, all of whom were fallible humans – always gave rise to doubt, for many religious dogmas appeared incredible. By contrast, reason led men to investigate questions objectively and anew, and – where arriving at a conclusion was possible – it produced consensus. Thus it may have been Paul who persuaded Khosro to investigate all the known faiths of his time in order to choose the best among them or, at least, to settle on a best combination of borrowings from them. I am not sure, however, what to make of Paul's other statement on Khosro, that the king "filled his head with the doctrines of Plato". Paul himself seems to have preferred firmly the doctrines of Aristotle over Plato's. In other words, he wanted us to arrive at our beliefs through evidence and demonstration, not prophetic authority or mystical visions. If so, his statement may well be a veiled criticism of his late patron's philosophical beliefs.

One last topic concerning philosophy under the Sasanians that deserves examining is the rise and suppression of Manichaeism in their territories, though the Great Kings failed to destroy the creed. As is well known, the religion thence spread to Arabia, Byzantium, North Africa and Chinese Turkistan, where it became the official religion of the Uigur empire for several centuries.   It also influenced the courses of philosophy and religion in subsequent ages elsewhere, as manifested most famously in St Augustine of Hippo's adherence to it in his first thirty years.

Māni was born in the second decade of the third century, apparently in a district near the capital, old Seleucia or Ctesiphon, on the Tigris. His father, who seems to have been a partner in his subsequent prophetic career, is said to have been born in Ecbatana – today's Hamadan in old Media – but had either converted in his youth to the Elkhasite brunch of Christian-Jewish Baptists in Babylonia, or else, entered the sect after marrying a Christian woman, possibly called Maryam, near Ctesiphon. When the boy was four years old, the family migrated further south in Babylonia to join the mainstream of the sect. Thus the child's native tongue became Aramaic, which was also the primary bureaucratic language of the empire. Later, he wrote in Middle Persian, particularly a treatise which he called Shāpūragān to present to Shāpūr in person. Māni himself says that he was twenty-four years old when Shāpūr ascended the throne, in 240AD, and it was about that time that he said he received his second revelation from an archangel. He had heard voices from early childhood. By Manichaean tradition, in his earliest youth he had told his father that he, his father, had begotten only his body. "Someone else entered it afterwards", he told him. This suggests a split personality syndrome. He had also told his father to point out the Elkhasites' doctrinal errors to them. The revelations caused his expulsion from the sect and he left for Ctesiphon in his early twenties, accompanied by two disciples and, later, his father.

Manichaean documents – which have survived in abundance in many languages, including Syriac, Parthian, Soghdian and Chinese – are moot on how he came across his seemingly deep knowledge of the main faiths of his world which he set out to perfect. But his preachings fell on fertile ground and he converted at least a few royal princes among the Sasanians, as well as some subordinate Parthian shahs elsewhere. He was no doubt helped by the disgust that many felt at the corruption that had afflicted the official Temple, and he practiced as a healer and physician. He claimed that he had the ability to transfer himself to distant parts of the world at will to give support to those of his supporters who needed it.

Manichaeism was a universalist creed that gave it an advantage over Zoroastrianism, in the sense that the latter had come to involve the believer in identifying with Iranian descent. Zoroastrianism did not, for example, appeal to Babylonians or Syrians or Byzantines, all of whom had their own, separate cosmogonies. By contrast, the new religion purported to combine the most attractive ethical principles of all the more prominent faiths of the empire grafted onto a Zoroastrian duality of God and the Devil for the benefit of the whole of Mankind. Further, Māni allowed his missionaries to pretend to believe fully in the religion of whatever locality in which they found themselves. They said that they believed even in the Homeric gods of the Greeks and Romans. Thus Māni called himself the Archangel of Light, preached the transmigration of souls – with his own soul being a reincarnation of Zeos, Zarathustra, the Budda and, particularly, Jesus as described by St. Paul. He taught eventual redemption in pure spiritual form in Zarathustra's Paradise.

Māni was an energetic organiser. As with St. Paul, he visited and wrote to his parish leaders frequently, and he funded the setting up of local missions wherever he could, particularly in his own, populous, Babylonia. He trained large numbers of scribes in various languages to translate and proliferate his teachings. Thus did the number of his followers expand rapidly. In Europe, it would reach Rome itself, and it would establish serious presences in Roman Egypt and Sasanian Arabia. I have already referred to its being the religion of St Augustine's youth in Hippo, in today's Tunisia. The Arabian branch proved important in the later shaping of Islam, for there are many parallels between the Manichaean model of prophesy and that of Muhammad four centuries later. Muhammad, too, received his mission to preach to the world from an archangel, and he, too, said that he was the "seal of all the prophets" that had gone before him.

Māni's cosmogony was, from the beginning, rooted in a thick layer of gloomy clay. He was a revolutionary who pretended to be only a mild reformer, and he often contradicted himself. It is said that he wrote so voluminously that he confused his disciples frequently. According to his world view, we humans had not been created by God, but by demons, to pollute God's creation as much as possible. After God had created the First Man, who

77

was his own son, the demons decided to create a sexual couple who would propagate themselves through insatiable copulation. All matter was evil and sexuality especially so.

Of course, every religion must also hold aloft a torch of hope for its adherents' eventual redemption, and so did Manicheism, in a most pretentious garb. The following quote from the Encyclopedia Iranica describes this aspect of the creed well:

> Although the world is made of demonic substance and is, as such, of an evil nature, … the redemption of the World Soul is the main object of cosmic history (human history included). The result of the cosmic history, however, is pre-determined by pre-cosmic events, the sacrifice of the First Man and the defeat of the demons at the hands of the Spirit of Life and the Mother of Life, even if the demons are not yet made powerless and even if the final divine victory will not be a perfect one.[19]

This is lavish enough nonsense to turn the head of a Schopenhauer, let alone the inhabitants of that impoverished, calamity-afflicted, pre-scientific age. Further, Māni's apparent disgust with the human body – he is himself believed to have been badly deformed – gave his teachings spiritual respectability. Māni was, in this sense, a successor to the ancient Sumerians, rather than to the largely-optimistic Indo-European newcomers on the Iranian plateau whom he emulated outwardly. Christianity and Islam would borrow from him heavily.[20]

---

[19] *Manicheism*: Encyclopedia Iranica Online, accessed January 2025.

[20] It is important not to give the impression that all Zoroastrians were optimists, or indeed that they were united in their interpretations of Zarathustra's hymns and prayers. The Sasanian ruling family are believed to have been ānites, a school of thought

The Sasanians, as we saw a little earlier, reached the height of their power and prestige under Khosro I in the sixth century. But they would not survive much longer. Less than a century later, they were swept away from a completely un-expected direction, by tribesman out of middle Arabia who had been united by a new religion but remained, as ever, hungry for loot and slaves. The last Sasanians exhausted themselves in their last ruinous war with the Byzantines, a war that lasted twenty-six years. Even though at times they reached Egypt, they ran out of resources and, further, their new weakness was noticed by the Arabs. Eventually, their armies, or what remained of them, lost the will to fight.

The Sasanian monarchy was an absolutist despotism, at least in its heartland of western Iran, though sometimes also elsewhere if the shāhānshāh in Ctesiphon was powerful enough to impose his/her will on all the vassal kingdoms in the provinces – mostly Parthians – and on the Zoroastrian priesthood. As for Sasanian society, in general, it too was divided – divided into several castes: the higher nobility, the priesthood, the village lords and, the lowest in rank, farmers, traders and artisans. The castes were formally hereditary, but, in real life, prone to the influence of wealth or even a forceful personality. One emperor, Wahrām V,

---

within Zoroastrianism that allocated a central role to Time, "ān" in Avestan. Accordingly, infinite Time and infinite Space had pre-existed Ahora Mazdā and his evil twin, Ahriman, and was an overpowering force in shaping our destinies. Thus did the ryal family's creed have a fatalistic tinge to it. By contrast, the regional courts of the subordinate shahs, most of whom retained their Parthian names, put little weight by the centrality of Time and can be said to have remained more classically Zoroastrian, believing strongly in free will. See the article *ānism* by Professor Albert de Jong in the Encyclopedia Iranica Online. The term ān has survived in modern Persian and Arabic as "zamān".

fell so thoroughly under the spell of his court musicians that he elevated them to the rank of the aristocracy. Marriage between the castes was frowned on, but again, exemptions were attained by the rich and powerful. Polygamy was practiced widely by the affluent, with wives subjected to a hierarchy of their own into four ranks presided over by a "king-wife". Slavery was similarly rife among those who could afford it and prisoners of war were routinely put to forced labour for life on royal estates, if they were not ransomed.

The whim of the emperor and his hereditary regional shahs being decisive most of the time, religious minorities, such as Jews, Christians and Manichaeans could be persecuted during one reign encouraged in the next. The love affair between at least one shāhānshāh, Khosro II, Parvīz, and his Christian, Armenian queen, Shīrīn, acquired legendary status in its own day and remains so throughout the Persianate world into our time.

Such rigidities did not necessarily mean that life for the average citizen or slave was worse than under neighbouring empires or states. It could even be better. Especially later under the Sasanians, law courts were omnipresent and the laws held in high repute. Neither were those laws that governed social life often so imprecisely defined as to leave them open to blatant mis-interpretation by corrupt judges, and they were not unusually repressive or cruel. For example, the minimum age of marriage for girls was fifteen years[21] and daughters could refuse

---

[21] More precisely, fourteen years and three months, for age was calculated on the assumption that the child had come into being at the moment of conception, nine months earlier. See Mahmoud Emami Namin: *The Legal Status of Women in the Sasanids' Era*: Cogent Arts & Humanities, 5:1, 1540962, DOI: 10.1080/23311983.2018.1540962.

the will of their fathers to marry men they did not love, though it risked being disowned by family. Women could own property separately, and the chief wife could succeed her husband as the next legal head of the family if the man did not have an adult male heir. In its last century, the dynasty even chose two female sovereigns. Nor could women be divorced at the whim of their husbands. Evidence had to be produced before a judge for the act to proceed, and wives had equal access to the courts to petition for divorce. Compared to what befell the Iranians when the empire fell to Islam – when the minimum age of marriage for females was reduced to eight years and nine months – nine lunar years — with men authorised to divorce any of their wives by merely uttering his decision three times, the depth of the subsequent disaster becomes clear.

The later Sasanians set up the first hospitals in the world – the present Arabic word for hospital being the Persian "bimārestān", and there were three great centres of learning in the land that are routinely described by today's historians as universities. Their memory and heritage would achieve lasting fame in Islamic times, as we shall see in the next chapter.

In terms of philosophical and theological change, the Sasanian era was of profound consequence, both for Zoroastrianism and the other major religions of the time. It bestowed governmental prestige and large sums of money on Zoroastrian temples, with their large retinues of theologians and priests, and encouraged them to become more learned in religion and philosophy. This was particularly true of the ānite school of thought within it, the school of thought to which the ruling family adhered. Further, as we saw above, it pursued and encouraged artists, thinkers and theologians from Byzantium and India to settle at its centres of learning. This was particularly true of Neo-Platonists who, in one famous citation, filled "Anushirwān's mind with the doctrines of Plato".

The development of Manichaeism and the rise of the communistic Mazdakite movement which some Great Kings embraced initially are other manifestations of the turmoil in ideas that was Sasanian Iran. As noted earlier, just one indication of the esteem in which Zoroastrianism was held abroad during the time of the later shāhānshāhs may be gleaned from the teachings of Gemistos Plethon some 900 years later. Plethon risked his life by advocating that Christianity be rejected in favour of a mixture of Zoroastrianism and an abstract interpretation of the gods of ancient Greece.

There remains hope that our knowledge of the Sasanians may yet deepen. Until recently, scholarship on the subject was largely confined to Westerners whose mastery of the Pahlavi, Arabic and Fārsi sources was limited. But now, mainly as a result of a large number of Iranian refugees settling at American and European universities, a new focus is being brought to bear on those sources. These Iranians are free of the disfavour imposed on their colleagues inside Iran by the present Islamic state there; yet they are understandably and fortunately sentimental about their pre-Islamic heritage. They have adequate sums of money at their command and they enjoy the freedom to travel internationally to meet and inspire one another. Consequently, their superior linguistic abilities and their patriotic motivation are producing sizable fruit. As the quote from Professor Sawer at the start of this chapter indicates, we are now witnessing a new era of research to remedy the neglect and shortcomings of the past.[22] In the next chapter or two, I shall examine the proposition

---

[22] As I write, I have in front of me a book of 450 pages in Persian that merely lists or describes briefly what remains, and what is said to have perished, of the writings of the Sasanians. Among these are

of modern scholars that the Abbāsid caliphate of Baghdad that played such an important part – however exaggerated – in the preservation of the Greek masters and their transmission to Europe, modelled itself on the Sasanian system. That new flowering could not have flourished without that recent memory.

---

not only what the Muslims later translated into Arabic – no doubt excising or even distorting whatever they found most unpalatable and destroying the original – but also a large body of religious and secular documents that were translated into Middle Persian, Avestan and Sanskrit by those Zoroastrian priests who fled to India and became known as the Parsees during the first four centuries of the Muslim era. Add to the list what has been metamorphosed by later poets into such literary works as the *Arabians Nights* or Ferdowsi's *Shāhnāmeh,* the latter of which to this day frustrates the efforts of Muslim activists to expunge them from the daily lives of Persians, Kurds, Afghans and Tajiks. See the *History of Iranian Literature Before Islam,* by Ahmad Tafazzoli. Tehran, 1997.

FIVE
The First Islamic States: Innocent pupils, but …

Coin of Mu'āwiyah I, the fifth caliph of Islam, depicting a Sasanian emperor with a Zoroastrian fire temple on the reverse and repeating the crescent moon-and-star emblem of the Persian crown[23]

Islam did not come naked into the world, and nor did its founder claim that he had brought a new faith to Mankind. It was a natural heir to the main religions of the region – as well as to previous Arab beliefs and practices. Indeed, the very word it uses

---

[23] This has to be a puzzle. Struck about 23 years after the last drachma coin of the last Sasanian emperor, only the name of the sovereign has been changed to that of Mu'āwiyah the caliph. The faithful imitation would have helped instant recognition of the value of the coin, but the designers and commissioners seem not to have realised that they were venerating some of the holiest concepts and emblems of the faith they had overthrown through violence.

85

for religion, "dīn", is borrowed from Sasanian Zoroastrianism and goes back some two millennia to the Avesta of Zarathustra himself. In the steps, too, of the last great prophet of the region, Māni, four centuries earlier, the new religion's divine mission was, it said, to correct and to improve upon all the known great religions of the region. In Māni's words, again, the prophet of Islam declared that he was "the seal2, the last and the finalisation of the prophets, after whom God would no-longer send any more messengers to humanity.

Inevitably, then, as the result of such a declaration, choices had to be made and judgements exercised. Which reforms or innovations should be chosen and which creeds would be the foremost models to emulate. Certainly, his audience was not wholly unfamiliar with the main pillars of faith of the competing, more sophisticated, previous religions. The Arabs of the Hijaz had long lived in the neighbourhood of Christian Arab kingdoms to the north and south, and sizeable groups of Jewish and Christian converts or immigrants lived among them. A brief look at Arabia's history before Islam will be instructive.[24]

Immediately to the east and north of the Hijaz for over three centuries had prospered the Arab kingdom of the Lakhmids. Outwardly, the House of Lakhm was a client kingdom of the Sasanians and often fought on their side against the Byzantines and the latter's own Arab client state in north-western Arabia and Syria, the Ghassānids. In truth, the Lakhmids were often left to their own ways and became assertive especially whenever the

---

[24] Fundamentalist Muslims routinely refer to pre-Islamic times as the *Jahelliyah* era, the era of ignorance. This is utter nonsense, of course, even in the hinterland of the Arabian desert, whose oases often acted as commercial way stations that linked the India Ocean to Europe and Egypt.

Sasanians and the Byzantines were locked in their long and exhausting wars. One future Sasanian emperor was even brought up at the Lakhmid court and the kingdom's capital, Hīra, on the Euphrates in Iraq, had a wide reputation among other Arabs for the wealth of its people and the fame of its poets, such as Nābighah al-Dhubiyāni. Unfortunately for Iran, emperor Khosro II, Parvīz – the only Sasanian ruler who had reached as far into the heart of Byzantium as to lay siege to Constantinople – brought the Lakhmids to an end when, around 602AD, he executed their last king, Nu'mān III, for rebellion. This caused such anger among the Arabs of the north-east and the Persian Gulf littoral that they rose against the mighty emperor and crushed a task force he sent against them. The Battle of Zīqār, as the decisive event became known, in effect ended Iranian rule in southern Iraq and north-eastern Arabia and gave the Arabs such confidence in themselves that their later overthrow of the empire became imaginable.

In other words, the Arabs were by then, not at all the savages that, under the influence of Ferdowsi in early eleventh century, many people today envisage them to have been:

Ze shire shotor khordano susmār,
Arab rā be jā'i rasidast kār
Ke tāje Kayān rā konad ārzu.
Tofu bar to ey Charkhe Gardun, tofu!

From camel milk lizard meat,
The Arab has now risen so high
That he eyes the crown of the Kays.
Spit upon you,
Oh, Wheel of Fortune,

87

In fact, decades before the rise of Islam, the Arabs of Iraq and northern Arabia had acquired some of the most modern weaponry of the time and acquired a deep knowledge of military strategy. As for what we might call "higher thought", both the Arab kingdoms of the north had become largely Christian, the Lakhmids had chosen the Nestorian variety that was acceptable to Iran, and the Ghassānids the Chalcedonian faith of the Romans. The slain Lakhmid king Nu'mān III had converted to Nestorianism in high ceremony.

Nor was the city of Mecca, in the interior of western Arabia, as desolate or impoverished a place as popularly imagined. Earlier, during the long periods of peace between the Sasanians and Byzantines, it had certainly fallen on hard ground. This was because, in peacetime, the more economical routes for east-west trade, such as the Euphrates valley in Mesopotamia and the Red Sea shipping lanes, thrived at the expense of the arduous, longer and more dangerous desert routes between the Persian Gulf and Syria. But latterly, the ruinous long war of 26 years between the two empires had resuscitated Mecca and made it a prosperous and vibrant city. As such, it had become the richest and the largest of its rivals.

Another change in the fortunes of Mecca that was to prove crucial was that a desert tribe, called the Quraish, had invaded it recently and replaced its native rulers to become the new dominant power of the region. Muhammad was born in around the year 570 AD into the clan of the Banu Hāshem within this

---

[25] Ferdowsi, who died in 1025, puts these words in the mouth of the commander of the Iranian army Rostam Farrokhzād as he faces the first Muslim attack.

tribe, but his immediate family were relatively poor – according to the few personal descriptions of him we find in the Koran – and, to make matters even more dire for him, both his parents died when he was an infant. He was taken in custody first by his aged grandfather and then, when he, too, died, by an uncle, Abu Tālib. Fortunately for him, the latter turned out to be a good man and a reasonably prosperous merchant who would take him along on his journeys from a young age, we are told.

Though Mecca had its communities of Jews and Christians, beside smaller groups of Zoroastrians and Manichaeans, most people appear to have been traditionally inclined. They worshipped their tribal gods in the shape of sacred stones, not necessarily out of conviction, but because the god of a clan or tribe symbolised its identity. Abandoning it in favour of another religion, even one of greater repute with a sophisticated and ancient theology, was regarded as an act of treason by the other members. Thus Mecca had also come to be a major religious centre, with a cubic building called the Ka'ba as the main gathering place of the sacred stones. A particular month was set aside for the annual visit of pilgrims from the peripherals, with fighting forbidden for the duration. The annual pilgrimage, in turn, helped further strengthen the economy of the city – as it does hugely still – and constituted yet another reason why the tribes and the clans were reluctant to give up their religions in favour of universalist creeds such as Christianity and Manicheism.

There is no reliable documentary evidence to suggest that Muhammad engaged in commerce, though a familiarity with trading terms in the Koran suggests that he did. Muslim Traditions of his life – though they began to surface some generations after his death and are therefore open to question – contend that from early in his youth he developed a reputation for honesty. As such, a rich widow by the name of Khadīja was attracted to him and employed him to manage her string of camels on the trade routes to Syria and, presumably, also to Iraq. He later married Khadījah and considered himself lucky. According to one verse in the Koran, God tells him: "Were thee not made rich [by me]"?

The tradition that says Muhammad in his youth and early manhood made many long caravan journeys to Syria is plausible and can serve to explain what we know of his subsequent life and career. During long months away from Mecca, he would have spent many a starry night on the floor of the desert in the company of fellow travellers who professed other faiths, and the conversation of Jews and Christians who claimed descent from Abraham – as did the Arabs – would have familiarised him with those faiths.

It is said that, in his spare time, Muhammad liked to retire to a cave near the city to meditate on his own, sometimes for a whole week or even longer. It is similarly believed by Muslims that he received his first revelation from the archangel Gabriel in such a wilderness when he was thirty years old (the same age as Zarathustra). He was ordered by Gabriel to "Iqra", to recite. To this he replied that he could not, for he was illiterate, only for the archangel to repeat the command, and suddenly the young man could. Thus was born the first chapter of the Koran, Qor'ān in Arabic, meaning "recitation". And the Recitation turned out to be of a resolutely monotheistic kind, declaring Allah, who had been only one prominent god among the many gods of Mecca, as the one alone to be worshipped hence, the one supreme creator of the world (as again with the command that Zarathustra received, in his case Ahora Mazdā). This new, more strictly monotheism god was that of the Jews, though not of the Christians, whose tangled Trinity – a single godhead in three manifestations – would have been hard to explain to his fellow tribesmen (as indeed it remains so to many of us today!).

Nevertheless, resistance there followed. At first, he preached his mission, which was to complete the chain of the prophets, to those he could trust. His wife Khadījah and his young cousin Ali ibn Abu Tālib were the first to believe him. Kind Abu Tālib followed. As he became more confident, Muhammed revealed his mission more widely and was cautioned by the leaders of his clan, the Banu Hāshem, who were custodians of the Ka'ba. As time went by and he ignored the admonitions, he was threatened with harsher punishments and some of his followers were beaten up. He persisted and sent some of his followers across the Red Sea to Ethiopia before sending others to the town of Yathrib to the north of Mecca. He followed the latter group a few years later.

In Yathrib – now called al-Madīnah (from Madīnaton Nabi – the City of the Prophet) – he was received well by sizable numbers of traditional-minded natives, but not those who had converted to Judaism or Christianity. These regarded him as an upstart and usurper, spelling trouble ahead for them.

The subsequent and rapid military rise of the new prophet to undisputed suzerainty over Mecca and the two Arab kingdoms of northern Arabia, indeed even the later bursting out of Muslim armies into the two great empires of the farther north soon after his death, need not detain us here. What is pertinent to this history is how the new creed was shaped during these years.

As already mentioned, Muhammad rejected Christianity's trinitarian manifestation of God, preferring Judaism's uncomplicated one-ness of the deity. With Zoroastrianism, he left alone its central belief in the transmigration of souls – reincarnation or metempsychosis – but took onboard its promise of life after death, including the full resurrection of the body in paradise, a day of judgement at the end of the world, free will, and the implied inability of God to be omnipotent in his struggles

91

against the devil Ahriman – here called Satan, as in Judaism – which is really a dualism, despite vehement denials by Zoroastrians, Jews and Muslims. In the steps of Māni, and Māni alone, he ascended to Heaven for a visit to the Divine Presence. The Muslim practice of five daily prayers bears a remarkable similarity to its Zoroastrian predecessor.[26]

To the Muslim believer, of course, these claims present not logical problem. It was natural for the last and most perfect of God's messengers to humanity to be privileged with the ability to stage the odd miracle to prove his authenticity, and it was natural that the faith should include the best doctrines and practices that Muhammad's predecessors had been told by God to preach on Earth. But the claims were bound to pose problems to future philosophers, such as Kindi, Fārābī, Avicenna and Averroes, who needed to be accepted as Muslims while also adhering to reason. We shall see in later chapters how each struggled in his own way to reconcile reason to revelation.

***

Muhammad was quite clearly a most remarkable personality. He was brave, he was resolute, and he was resourceful, his strong nerves seemingly forged in the grievous losses that he suffered during his childhood. He also developed a grand vision for his people that would improve their status in the region and make them prosperous. But outsiders may judge that he lost some rare

---

[26] The Zoroastrians, as with today's Muslims, stood up to pray, with their hands raised, except that they faced the sun or a source of light. The earliest Muslims in Yathrib (Madīnah) stood towards Jerusalem, from which Muhammad said he rose the Divine Presence in Heaven on the back of an archangel. A little later, he made Mecca the holist city of Islam.

opportunities, too. Of that more in a moment. He envisaged for the Arabs of Mecca and the regions around it a monotheistic faith that competed in sophistication with the established creeds, chiefly Judaism and Christianity, and was yet simple enough to be readily understood by the man in the town square or the Bedouin in his tent. He codified the laws that governed relationships between those he addressed, and he based those laws on a clear set of ethical precepts that were not unfamiliar to them. His philosophy of governance, however, was a totalitarian one, along the lines of Plato's Republic, but perhaps even more authoritative. He divided the world into two Manichaean opposites, Dāral Islam and Dārel Harb, the House of Submission, submission to Allah, and the House of War, all others. His ideal state revolved around a single, all-powerful philosopher king whose loss or lapse risked instant disintegration, as indeed occurred with his own unexpected death at the age of 62. His successors quickly resorted to plots and assassinations and fell into a civil war that resulted in a cynical hereditary monarchy replacing them within only a couple of decades. He also failed to carry out much needed social reforms. It can be argued that after he captured Mecca in January 630 and achieved undisputed power, he could have mitigated the rules that governed slavery and the status of women. Perhaps he did not live long enough to do so, for he died only two-and-a-half years after the capture of Mecca. He did, however, tell his followers that slaves and women were human beings and that God looked favourably on those who treated them well. He left the institutions themselves unchanged.

On Muhammed's death, his closest companions chose his eldest father-in-law, Abu Bakr, to succeed him with the title Caliph meaning Deputy, deputising for Allah on Earth, that is. But Abu Bakr died only two years later, upon which another father-in-law and one of his other oldest companions, Umar ibn Khattab, was chosen. Umar lasted ten years and presided over the spectacular conquest of the bulk of the Byzantine Empire and the whole of the Sasanian, but he succumbed to a Persian slave's dagger. The next two caliphs also died in assassinations, by which time disagreements on the right path forward and the ambitions of tribal leaders whose conversion to Islam had never been quite sincere but motivated by the prospect of loot plunged the new empire into a civil war that ended in a formal monarchy.

The four first caliphs are generally grouped together by Muslims as the Rāshidūn caliphs, the Rightly Guided ones, but even with them, their behaviour was often quite ungodly. Their pursuit of booty and slaves in the conquered lands disturbed even some of their own people, and their armies routinely beheaded large numbers of captured soldiers after battles. Before late, however, the stability that they created in the vast regions under them – and their extolling of the merchant on the model of Muhammad's own example – resulted in a political entity that was one of the largest trading empires that the world had seen previously.

One specific charge of cultural barbarism commonly laid at the door of Umar, the second caliph, however, can be ruled out with confidence, though barbarism nevertheless did occur under him and his three next successors. It says that he ordered the destruction of the great library of Alexandria by replying to his commanders there that if it contained any truthful information, it would be surplus to the Koran, while if it contained untruths, it would be harmful. In either case, it better be destroyed. It is now known that the library had burnt down previously under the Byzantines. But many lesser libraries did indeed perish. One example is the royal library in Ctesiphon. The great city and its many suburbs were abandoned by their inhabitants in 637 in haste, leaving vast amounts of treasure to the invaders. The City's Royal Library, its large university and an unknown number of private collections possessed countless books of history, literature, theology and philosophy whose names only have survived in later Persian, Syriac and Arabic reports. No doubt many have not survived even in name. Ctesiphon was looted a second time under Ali, the fourth caliph, by fundamentalist soldiers who rebelled against him for not being tough enough against his enemies.

A similar fate befell the other two renowned Sasanian centres of learning, the complex of colleges in Gondishāpūr in southern Persia and in Nisibis on the border with Byzantine Anatolia. It is possible that some of the destruction was not intentional, but antagonism towards them there certainly was, perhaps specially widespread among the initial invading warriors. All non-Arabic literature left behind by the former enemies – now seen as heathens – was suspected of being refutations of Islam, and as the previous era was now labelled formally as the Ayyām el Jāhiliyah, the Days of Ignorance, and writing that might reflect well on it challenged the label. However, simple, unintended neglect was equally damaging. There was no enthusiasm to spend money on preserving books and records in the strange languages of the vanquished. They could be allowed to wither.[27]

In the year 661, Ali, the fourth, caliph was assassinated and the first civil war of the new empire came to a formal end when the

---

[27] Hostility to pre-Islamic Iran continues among some Muslim Iranians today, under the present Islamic Republic. May archaeological sites have been vandalised or allowed to suffer through neglect. In one case after the Islamic revolution of 1979 in the Kurdish city of Qasre Shīrīn, a Muslim zealot boasted to a brother of mine how he had used a bulldozer to destroy a Sasanian ruin. My brother had the courage to call him a "traitor". "Barbarian" would have been a more accurate term, for the man meant well.

challenger, Muāwiyah, the governor of Syria and a noble-born potentate of the Arabs of Mecca, took over as the new ruler. He transferred the capital from austere Kūfah in southern Mesopotamia to soft, civilised, still-largely-Christian Damascus and made the succession openly monarchical. The opulence of his new dynasty, the Umayyads, began. After him, his son Yazīd I, put down a revolt by Ali's second son Hussein with extreme cruelty and the future forking of Islam into its present division between Sunnis and Shiites became inevitable, with the bulk of the unhappiness among the Shiites of Iran, no doubt partly also due to the Iranians' inability to forgive the Arabs for their original sin, the destruction of the old empire.

Muāwiyah was in some respects a better man than were the Rightly-Guided caliphs. He was no zealot and retained some of the codes of chivalry that had been observed by his ancestors. My favourite story of his reign has a young man coming to his regular open majlises, when any citizen could ask to meet him to raise a grievance. The young man first caused discomfort when he sat down without being invited to do so by the caliph. He then told Mu'āwiyah that he wished to marry his widowed mother. The caliph pretended to be amused and asked why. His mother, he said, was a very old women, without a single tooth in her mouth. The young man replied that it did not matter. He had heard that she had a wide bottom and he fancied women with wide bottoms. The caliph kept his temper. He replied that it was up to his mother. He would report the young man's request to her and let him know.

Mu'awiyah had by then established firm roots in Syria. He had a large army there and, with the help largely of local Christian experts, had set up a sizeable bureaucracy for the collection of revenue and other functions of a state. Thus did his transfer of the capital there make sense. Damascus was centrally situated between Egypt in the west and Iran in the east, and it was advanced in every expertise a ruler needed. It also had a better climate than did appallingly hot and dusty southern Iraq.

Muāwiyah's brood went on to furnish the new empire with thirteen more caliphs over the following century and took Islam into Spain in Europe and into the borderlands of China. But although the rulers called themselves caliphs and pretended to deputising for God on Earth, they went the way of all previous absolute monarchies. They began as patriotic or clannish Arabs, but political and economic necessity and the urges of the flesh caused them quickly to relax the rules. Though at first none of their sons would quality for the succession if born to a non-Arab woman, by their final decades, they were sometimes indistinguishable from Byzantines. The last caliph was the blue-eyed son of a Kurdish slave woman, though perhaps "concubine" would be a better description.

Under the Umayyads, the new Muslim state produced no philosophical work of note. Its leaders were too busy warding off plots or conquering new lands to dream of abstract thought. Building cool palaces in deserts and adorning cities with new cathedral mosques were more to their liking, though there was certainly no shortage of philosophers from among the Christians, Jews and Zoroastrians who volunteered to bring intellectual glitter to their courts. Some of these even converted to Islam to endear themselves to the new masters.

Marwān II, the blue-eyed last Umayyad caliph, was overthrown in 750 by an army commanded by a Persian general and nearly all possible claimants to his throne murdered, with the notable exception of one prince who managed to reach Spain and was accepted there as the legitimate heir.

A main factor behind the upheaval resulted probably from how the Umayyads looked upon their subjects. Under them, converts to Islam, and even the sons of Arab men who had been born to

97

non-Arab mothers, were not given the equal rights that the prophet had promised all Muslims. Converts were called the Mawāli, meaning "clients", but it was really a euphemism for "owned" or, at most, contracted servants. The Mawāli were free to prosper in the professions, but only as members of the households of men of Arab birth. But as their numbers increased and they acquired wealth and influence, so did deepen their resentment against Damascus. In the distant, huge province of Khorāsān in north-eastern Iran and central Asia, eventually, they found their chance.

But, as already hinted, another font of resentment in Iran was lingering folk memory humiliation and suffering in the original conquest two centuries earlier. For example, though officially a Shia Muslim, the general who led the revolt is said to have been born with the Zoroastrian names of Behzādān, son of Vendād Hormozd. Presumably after conversion to Islam, or the pretence of it, he was named Abu Muslim Khorāsāni.

Yet another indication of that resentment may be the fact that the Persian slave, Pirūz Nehāvandi, who had assassinated Umar – the caliph who had overseen the invasion of Iran – quickly became an Iranian national hero, with a shrine built in his honour in his purported city of birth.[28]

Be that as it may, the new regime wasted little time before it diluted its ties with its Iranian, mainly Shiite, kingmakers. A mere five years into its success, it lured its Abu Muslim to Iraq and murdered him at a dinner party thrown in his honour. The new caliphs, leaders of the Bani Abbās clan, were distant relatives of the prophet and, as with the Umayyads, chose at first

---

[28] The shrine has survived into our time and every year attracts pilgrims from among Shia Muslims on the anniversary of his act, the day being called Omar-Koshān, Umar-Killing.

to endear themselves to their fellow Arabs. They also thought it prudent to side with the majority sect, orthodox Sunnism. Other changes followed quickly. The capital was transferred back to Iraq, the base of the Abbasid clan, and a new capital built on the site of an old Persian village on the Tigris called Baghdad.

But the new regime, too, being an absolute monarchy, soon began to go the decadent way of its predecessor and developed a taste for luxuries acquired through harsh taxation. By the time of the fifth caliph, the fabled Hārūn ar-Rashīd, the state had been transformed from a sincere theocracy into an imperium of outlandish splendour, though it was not as secure as some historians have depicted it. Rebellions rose in every direction – as indeed they had under the Umayyads – from distant north Africa and Egypt to central Asia and beyond. Even fratricidal wars became normal. Survive, however, the new empire of Baghdad did, and vastly expanded trade made it even more opulent. Hārūn could afford to send a gift elephant across Europe to far-off Frankia's Charlemagne. His merchants, aided by the usefulness of Arabic, Persian, Latin, Soghdian and Chinese, operated in all the three continents and brought back furs from Scandinavia and silken clothes from China. White European children made a particularly lucrative commodity and large numbers of Africans were imported to work on farms, particularly in Iraq, where they would later stage a series of significant rebellions.

The overall record is not as disturbing as perhaps suggested here. There were achievements, too. The technique of making paper was learnt from Chinese merchants in central Asia and handed over, eventually, to Europe. Modern numerals, too, including the number 0, were acquired from India and revolutionised mathematics with huge long-term consequences for the whole of the world.

Politically and in modes of administration, the new caliphate "was a revival of the Sasanian Empire", says Professor Touraj Daryaee, one of our contemporary specialists in the history of that era, because "The Sasanian Empire [had been] a unification of the Iranian and Mesopotamian core civilisations and when Islam entered the picture, it had no choice but to follow its model in many respects".[29]

The Abbāsids, more than the Umayyads, clung to the principle of the indivisibility of the ruler and the priest. It had been the reason why they had been promoted over the Umayyads. But in 813, there arrived on the throne a philosopher king, a prince who believed that the Koran had been created in time and therefore had dated in time. The implication was that the holy book had served its purpose, though such a phrase was never used. It shook the clerical class. The Deputy of Allah on Earth was invoking a foreign concept to undermine Islam. It was true and it appears as if it goes back all the way to Heraclitus's advocation of all phenomena being subject to change in time, but it may well have been borrowed from those Sasanians next door again, and they traced it back all the way to Zarathustra's Avesta. In that holy book, Time, Zurwān, was a minor, yet powerful, deity at whose feet we all fell, eventually.

The new philosopher king, Ma'mūn, was Hārūn's son and the seventh Abbāsid ruler. Among his Arab critics, he had acquired the nickname "Persian Boy" on account of his mother being an Iranian slave and on his own account of spending many years during his childhood and youth as the Governor of Khorāsān. There, his main philosophy tutor had been a Zoroastrian of noble

---

[29] *Sasanian Persia: The Rise and Fall of an Empire.* I. B. Tauris, London, 2009, p xvi.

birth and so enamoured was he of Khorāsān that, after becoming caliph, he refused to move to Baghdad for eight years.

Towards the end of his reign, Ma'mūn became even more obstinate on the truth of his philosophical beliefs. He flogged and imprisoned any learned doctor of the faith who disagreed with him or questioned his favoured theology, the theology of Mu'tazilism – those who had withdrawn [from taking sides between the Alīds and the Umayyads]. But the label had by then become a misnomer. Mu'tazilism was no-longer about the legitimacy of recent rulers. In the previous century, it had developed into a philosophical school and raised the ire of the orthodox, such as the literalist Ash'arites. Whereas the orthodox advocated the uncreatedness of the Koran, its being God's knowledge and therefore always present with him, the Mu'tazilites referred to specific recent events and persons in the holy book to conclude that it could not be as old as God.

The new theology had been instilled in Ma'mūn by his tutors and other sages in Khorāsān and these he promoted in his father's Bayt al Hikmah, House of Wisdom, in Baghdad, when he became caliph himself. Many secular books had already been translated into Arabic from Greek, Middle Persian, Syriac and Sanskrit. New works were added, consisting mainly of mathematics, astronomy, astrology, medicine, etc. More purely philosophical works were added to the tally, and the academy – originally a library only – was thrown open to linguists, theologians and philosophers who openly advocated the superiority of Zoroastrianism, Judaism and Christianity to Islam. Thus did Ma'mūn's Baghdad become a haven of free speculation. In the city there thrived even a social club that barred Arabs from membership, reasoning that they were racially inferior to the Persians and Romans. Needless to say, the caliph's persecution of the traditional clericy acquired a name of its own among the disgruntled: the Mihnah, the Inquisition or

101

Ordeal, as officials and theologians were told to submit to deep questioning on what they believed. Opposition to the heretical caliph went underground in city and country alike.

But Persian Boy was strong and determined and the enforcement of his philosophy lasted over two more reigns, altogether for almost two decades until, 851. As a result, by the time it was reversed by a new deeply devout caliph with equal cruelty, its seeds had reached all the provinces, and freethinking thrived. This new love of the ancients becomes clear in the next chapter when I examine the life and writings of Al-Kindi, the first Arab philosopher to deserve the description.

In concluding this introduction, I have to say that many Western commentators on the new flowering of philosophy under the Abbāsids, as opposed to the practical and useful sciences, have allowed their enthusiasm for their study to overcome their better counsel. Basically, Islam, as with all religions with a set of inviolable doctrines and a unified clericy, found – and still finds – freethinkers an existential threat. With the exception of times when a particular ruler has felt strong enough to ignore his official temple, as was the case of Ma'mūn, this suppression of descent has been the rule, not the exception. This is despite the Koran's explicit injunction ordering Muslims to seek "ilm", knowledge, wherever it can be found, "*Otlebol elm, walow bes-Sīn*", "seek knowledge even onto China". This is because the injunction does not really mean what it conveys today at face value. "Ilm" at that time meant technical skills such as medicine, engineering, architecture, particularly the manufacturing of weapons. Even today, "ilm" has come exclusively to mean science, not wisdom. From the very start, all knowledge that might cast doubt on Koranic cosmogony was banned vehemently. No rigid ideology with interests vested in power tolerates suggestions that it is based on false claims. I can imagine the prophet of Islam himself tolerating, for example, the

102

classification of fossilised remnants of ancient animals which were a famous curiosity in his time. But if any such research led people to think that our species had not come into being whole, that the story of Adam and Eve was but tribal make-belief, the perpetrator would have instantly been expelled from the gatherings of the faith and made to suffer the consequences.

What complicated matters was that the early centuries of Islam were its age of innocence. The new faith had emerged from a playful polytheism of many brands and therefore required time to wake up fully to the implications of its own new doctrines. Nor did the new state in its first years possess instruments of repression sufficiently sophisticated to enforce orthodoxy everywhere. As a result, the early Muslims proved eager pupils. They were eager to hear alternative stories of the creation, the other possible explanations of the world and of human life. With the passage of time and, especially, the gradual coming into being of a professional priesthood to police official doctrine, the horizons began to close in.

SIX

Kindi, the Arab

*"The Writer of Baghdad" – Kindi as celebrated in 1962
on an Iraqi postage stamp. The real man seems to have been
a much more assertive personality than this pious recluse depicts him.*

As pointed out earlier, the famous Bayt al-Hikma or House of Wisdom translation institute in Baghdad was not founded by the freethinker caliph al-Ma'mūn, but his father, the famously swashbuckling Hārūn, and my favourite story of the latter

105

depicts him, officially God's Deputy on Earth, as a sultan who felt secure enough on his throne not to mind projecting an ungodly image of himself. It says that one day, a bard was allowed into his audience hall to recite a ballad he had composed in praise of his extensive conquests. Hārūn was pleased – or pretended to be pleased – and ordered that the poet's mouth be filled with as many gold coins as it could receive. It was a big mouth and the man left the palace elated beyond his dreams, only for him to be set upon by the caliph's servants immediately outside the hall and forced to disgorge his hard-earned reward. There was little he could do, but hope that he would have a second chance to see Hārūn to tell him what wicked men had come to surround him and give him a bad name. This did come about, eventually, in a wilderness, when Hārūn was out hunting. "Oh, Great Deputy of Allah", he addressed the mounted sovereign, before describing his misfortune. The reply was not what he expected. "Well, my good man", Hārūn replied, "You said something you didn't mean, and so did we".

The arrogance had obviously become hereditary in the House of Abbās, for, as we have seen, Hārūn's second son and successor Ma'mūn would flog and imprison even the highest-ranking clerics of the land if they questioned his philosophy even mildly, and so Ma'mūn became the patron of the Arabs' first native philosopher.

Abu Yūsef Ya'qūb ibn Ishāq al-Kindi was born around the year 805 AD the son of an aristocrat and climbed the ladders into the innermost sanctums of the caliphal family, but died some 68 years later in official disgrace.

Kindi was a descendent of the kings of Kinda, in eastern Arabia and his father was appointed the governor of a city in southern Iraq. In Kūfah and, later in Baghdad, he grew up to become "jack of all trades, master of none", to use that telling English phrase.

106

He became a philosopher, but one who would soon be almost completely forgotten. The fate is undeserved, perhaps precisely because he mastered no specialism. He was prolific in his writing and devoted his life to spreading the wisdom of the ancients.

Although there is no indication that he supported the persecution of the Mu'tazilites by Ma'mūn, his mere attachment to the court caused voices to be raised against him early. Indeed, it would have been sufficient for raising the ire of the orthodox if one merely peddled the thinking of foreigners, or whatever was not in the Koran. As an ambitious young man wishing to endear himself to famous intellects, he would have known some of the most glittering names that have come down to us from the Bayt such as Khwārazmi, the mathematician who gave his name to the logarithm, that beloved word of today's computer search engines. (Khwārazmi ought perhaps to be regarded as the single greatest thinker of the era, for his mathematical innovations laid the foundations not only for rapid new progress in that subject, but, also, indirectly, for later achievements in rationalist and empirical philosophy. He is the first known user of Indian numerals in the Islamic world, including the revolutionary digit zero,[30], and he invented the word algebra[31].)

When Mu'tazilism was abandoned by the caliph Mutawakkil and there came the turn of the orthodox to suppress their critics, Kindi's library was confiscated, though it is said that its more innocuous volumes were returned to him. It is also said that he was beaten.

Judging by a small minority of his writings that have survived, we might describe Kindi as an essayist, for rarely does he dwell at length on a particular topic to explain quite why he reaches his conclusions. However, the enthusiasm that he helped to create among the new intelligentsia outlived the persecution of the freethinkers and bore fruit in future generations. For many years his main responsibility was to supervise one of the two groups of full-time translators at the Bayt – the other supervisor being the Nestorian Christian Abu Zaid Hunayn ibn-Ishāq at-Ibādi who is reported to have spoken Greek, Syriac and Persian beside Arabic – and, at court, Kindi tutored senior princes. Altogether, some 250 pieces of writing are listed in Kindi's name by a

---

[30] His Iranian background in the country of Khwārazm in central Asia must tempt one to ask if Indian numerals had not already been in use in late Sasanian times. See the reign of Khosro I, above, who sent researchers to India to find and translate into Middle Persian the best works of literature, science and wisdom of that ancient civilisation. The evidence may well have disappeared in the upheaval of the Arab conquest. Tabari, the Iranian-born historian of the next generation in Baghdad, gives "al-Majūsi" – meaning "the Zoroastrian" – as his second epithet, suggesting that he either still adhered to the old faith, or else, had converted to Islam in his middle years.

[31] Derived from the word jabr for "forcing" or "making inevitable".

contemporary bookseller, the great majority of which are of a non-philosophical nature. They range from mathematics and optics to weather prediction based on the Koran. Only about 40 of his works have survived and many of these are in a poor state of decay and lend themselves to various readings.

Al-Kindi's most influential philosophical work, which illustrates the severe restriction of philosophical development under all theocracies, is his Metaphysics or First Philosophy, a long commentary on what he, wrongly, attributes to Aristotle. It sets out to prove that Koranic cosmogony, prophethood and the other basic doctrines of Islam can be derived from reason, according to Aristotle. (All Muslim philosophers, that is, all those who have been convinced sincerely of the truth of Islam, have suffered from – and been diminished by – this desire to reconcile reason and revelation.) But it was a good beginning in Kindi for Muslims. He urged them to reject any claim that contradicted reason or evidence, though it is also fair to say that he himself did not always abide by his advocacy. He is quoted as saying:

> We must not shirk the truth but seek it anywhere we can find it, from even races and nations who are different from us. Nothing ought to be dearer to the seeker after truth than truth itself. Truth does not diminish he who discovers it or transfers it to others.

Kindi was a firm Mu'tazilite and made some valuable contributions of his own to the philosophy of his region. The literalists, such as the Ash'arites and the Hanbalites, were thus right to take fright at him and his kind. Their advocacy meant that if a single sentence of the Koran did not make sense or seemed unjust or unkind, the whole of the holy book came under suspicion as either corrupted or not the revelation of a good God.

Alongside the Mu'tazilites, but contrary to Aristotle –without Kindi himself knowing it – he believed that God had created the world out of nothingness, ex nihilo, and that God, the First Cause

109

Without Cause, had existed before Time, for he was the cause of Time, as well as all else. God could also uncreate the world. The world and all else were thus finite; only God the creator was infinite.

Kindi opposed attributing any qualities to God, the Frist Cause, for God was utterly singular, unlike all other entities that were multiple in their constituent parts. This is, of course, an absurd criterion for distinguishing between entities, and it is, by the way, a contradiction. Is singularity itself not an attribute, and how does he know that the First Cause is a singularity? But his thinking that we must avoid any description of an ultimate first cause of existence remains interesting in that it perhaps hints at the irresolvability, the illogicality, of why anything exists at all. If this reading of him is justified – and in this he merely parrots some of the ancients – the suggestion is gaining ground once more.[32]

Of Kindi's First Philosophy only the first part of four sections remains, in a single manuscript in Istanbul, but the sections are detailed enough to convey the essence of his metaphysics. He sets out to prove that Greek philosophy is superior to all others, that the world is created and finite, and that a First Cause or The True One, as he calls it, has to exist by necessity. He identifies the True One with Allah.

Fil Falsafa al-Ulā, or, On First Philosophy, is dedicated to Ma'mūn's son and successor Mu'tasim, whose son Ahmad he

---

[32] See this writer's *The Ultimate Question: In search of God in a godless universe*, 2024. Kindi, as with numerous others, calls the potential, the First Cause that must exist by necessity, "God". This writer discourages any use of that term for in ordinary language and in many cultures, "God" has many precise attributes, such as knowledge, agency and intention.

was tutoring at the time. Its opening passages are not without stylistic charm and immediately set the tone for the rest of the work[33]:

> Oh, son of the most noble among nobles, and of the strongest beneficiaries of bliss. I ask Allah for a long survival for you. May He adorn you with all the rewards of virtue and spare you all that is base in nature, for whoever abides by the right path is the surely the happiest of men, both in the realm of this world and of the other, the eternal.

> [Know that] the highest among all the arts is the art of philosophy, the pursuit of the true knowledge of things, as far as it is possible for man to achieve. It is the aim of the philosopher to seek the truth and to act according to that truth. ... But he will not find that truth if he seeks it without first finding its cause; and the cause of the existence and continuance of all things is the True One.[34] Everything that exists has truth, but the True One exists necessarily, and all things that exist owe their existence to Him. ...

Thus in Kindi's writing, the foundation of philosophy is the pursuit of the knowledge of God. Were it not for the extremely long chain of thinkers, both before and after him, Jewish, Christian and Muslim alike, who set the same aim for themselves, declaring first the truth of prophetic claims before trying to arrive at them through reason, we should regard Kindi as no more than a theologian. In this respect, the world of Islam continues to remain behind him (Whereas in Christianity it would be hard today to find any respected philosopher who still speaks of God as the conscious creator of the world depicted by

---

[33] My translation, slightly compressed and not always verbatim.

[34] In the late sixth or early fifth century BC, Xenophanes called it "The One", but it seems unlikely that Kindi would have heard of Xenophanes. His source is most likely to be the Neo-Platonist Plotinus.

Paul, Augustine or Aquinos, the practice remains universal in Islamic philosophy. I cannot, for example, at present envisage a Muslim theologian finding a publisher that would be the Muslim equivalent of Don Cupitt's Taking Leave of God (1980) or Bishop Jack Spong's Why Christianity Must Change or Die (1998).)

Of Kindi's other philosophical writings that have survived, perhaps the most important is his essay On the Number of Aristotle's Books. This is because it includes a compendium of philosophical terms that had in recent times been imported into Arabic from Greek and other languages. In this, and in the steps of Cicero who "gave the Romans philosophy" by bringing Greek philosophical terms into Latin or picking Latin equivalents for them, Kindi and his predecessors in the Translation Movement who really date back to the Omayyad dynasty, gave Arabic a philosophical lexicon that made possible the writings of the later, more influential, Arabic-language philosophers, such as Fārābī and Avicenna. Nor did the beneficiary languages stop at Arabic. The terminology continues to be used in the other tongues of the world of Islam, such as New Persian or Fārsi, Turkish, Indonesian and Urdu.

Before we move on, however, a note ought also to be made of a significant failure of the Arabic translation movement. Beside its undoubted achievements, it inflicted lasting damage on the subsequent development of philosophy among Muslims by assigning some of the works of the classical writes to others, particularly the works of the Neo-Platonists to Aristotle. Aristotle, for example, believed that the world was not created, that it was eternal, and that God was merely an artisan manager of the world. Totally erroneously, Kindi and his colleagues labelled their own borrowings from such Neo-Platonists as Plotinus, Porphyry and Proclus, even some Christian Church Fathers, as "the theology of Aristotle". Later on still, as some of

112

the original works in Greek and Latin disappeared, their Arabic translations were the only version left. Some of the translations were also inaccurate, in some cases edited so as not to contradict Islamic doctrine. In these cases, where the originals have disappeared, the damage continues, while where the originals have survived, largely in locked chests in Byzantine monasteries or private libraries, it took ages for the inaccuracies or distortions to be discovered. On the whole, though, the Abbāsid translation effort remains a significant contribution to the history of philosophy.

Finally, perhaps we should stress once more that the rumpus of noises that was the philosophical movement of Abbāsid Baghdad included some brave dissenters, and that, in Baghdad, a recently-founded city no-larger than a large town, the literate elite mingled intimately, and that Kindi and his respectable colleagues would have been fully familiar with the views of anyone else who had any view. This may help us to put the philosophers under discussion in this survey in context and even provide us with some clues to their thinking. To what extent were they affected by one another's contentions? Thus let me describe briefly two such figures whom Kindi must have known personally, for both were active Mu'tazilites in Baghdad during his middle years. They renounced all religions in strong terms and attacked Islam in particular.

The first of the pair was an Arab by the name of Abu Isā Warrāq ("the paper maker") who was executed a dozen years or so before Kindi died. After leaving Mu'tazilism, he is said to have become a Shiite activist before giving up that sect, too, in favour, reputedly, of Manichaeism, for one contemporary historian described him as "a secret Zindīq". This, however, may not be a proof. The term "Zandik" had begun in Sasanian Persian as a term of abuse against Manichaeans, but had come by this time in Arabic to mean a heretic in general, and a a heretic the Paper-

113

Maker certainly was. He wrote a book called Maqālāt or Articles in which he denounced all prophets as magicians and all miracles as staged or erroneous perceptions. He was particularly bitter against the prophet of Islam.

The other famous dissenter was Warrāq's Iranian-born student and disciple who fled the clutches of the executioner. He seems to have been only slightly younger than his master, for he died shortly after Warrāq's slaying, by which time he is said to have written 114 books. He was called Abul-Hasan Ahmad Ibn Rāwandī and gave some of his works startlingly daring titles. One was called Against the Koran and described the holiest document of Islam as "neither revealed nor even a work of literary merit". All miraculous tales about the prophet that were ascribed to his companions in the hadīth, he said, had been made up by them because they had a vested interest in the success of the new religion. His accusers described him as an outright atheist, adding that he hid behind his denial of God's existence by saying that he was merely quoting Indian brahmins. None of his books have survived to enable us to judge him with confidence, but his critics have quoted generously enough of them to give us a fairly detailed picture.

This other side of Baghdad ought not to be ignored, for both these men, and no doubt many others among their colleagues whose names have not come down to us, were products of the Translation Movement, equally, and can help us to assess better the voices that we examine next, among whom must be Fārābī, a ranking philosopher whatever our view of his conclusions.

SEVEN

Fārābī the Soghdian

Contested national hero of several modern states: Fārābī as imagined for a postage stamp in Kazakhstan in 1993, after the fall of Communism.

In reading any important philosopher, but most of all in reading Aristotle, it is necessary to read him in two ways: with reference to his predecessors, and with reference to his successors. In the former aspect, Aristotle's merits are enormous; in the latter, his demerits are equally enormous. For his demerits, however, his successors are more responsible than he is.
Bertrand Russell[35]

Why were many pre-scientific wisemen – in other words pre-modern philosophers – so keen to discover how to transmute base metals into gold? A huge flaw in their calculations, and in their morality, which must have been obvious to themselves, was that if they succeeded, the knowledge might, and probably would, leak quickly outside their secret cabals and make gold

---

[35] *History of Western Philosophy,* Chapter 19, Aristotle's metaphysics.

worthless. Their immorality stemmed from their expectation that, in the shorter term, it would make them rich. Fārābī was one such seeker. On the other hand, he refused to make money from astrology in which he did not believe, which is a credit to him in that intensely superstitious age, including among the idle rich who were his patrons. On the whole, though, one is tempted to suspect that many such philosophers knew in their hearts that they were fraudsters, that they were no better than the quack doctors they denounced frequently. Only a century after Fārābī, one of their own rank, Omar Khayyām of Nishāpūr, an equally avowed Aristotelian and admirer of Socrates, would write:

> The stars roaming far-flung skies
> Have come to belong to the haughty Wise!
> My son, listen well. This is my finding:
> The Wise themselves know they philosophise![36]

And yet, long into posterity, even in this age of the triumph of science when we manufacture diamonds on an industrial scale, we continue to refer to such philosophers as great thinkers. In truth, if they were alive today to see how we fetched a little box out of a pocket and used it to speak to friends on the other side of the world, they would feel humiliated by the extent of their primitiveness as compared to our children. The best practice has to be, at least in the case of the sincere among the pre-scientific philosophers, that we allow for their scientific ignorance and ask ourselves what *we* would have done if we had been in their place.

Here is another question. Does it matter where a philosopher hails from? Ideally, it ought not to. The pursuit of knowledge is supposed to be objective and we would not ask such a question

---

[36] My translation. See *Omar Khayyām: Poet, Rebel, Astronomer,* 2007, p. 287.

of a chemist or geologist. While chemists wishing to discover, say, the structure of the atom of magnesium, will eventually converge on a particular set of facts, no-matter which part of the world they inhabit and no matter how isolated from one another they might be, philosophers will rarely come to precise agreement on the subjects of their study, even when working together. The subjects of their inquiries are not how many subatomic particles – or "waves" – there might be in a neutron. They look into questions that may not even have answers on which we may agree, or no answers at all. Are humans good or bad, for example, and good or bad from whose point of view. What is "good" or "bad", anyway, and what do we mean by human nature? Further, the answers we may provide to such questions are affected by our upbringing, our cultures, our ethnic identities, even perhaps by the landscape and the climate of our homelands. In this light alone, therefore, I think that it is relevant to ask to which people and to which land a particular philosopher belongs. Russell, the universal face of humanism in the middle years of the twentieth century, and perhaps for many centuries to come, used to remind his admirers that he was "passionately English".[37]

This question of ethnicity may have another benefit in any study of philosophy in the world of Islam. It may hint at why, after Kindi – who was really more of a theologian than a philosopher – all notable thinkers within Islam rose in other regions than the faith's heartland of Arabia and Iraq, and why they tend to distance themselves – as far as they dare – from the prophethood of Muhammad.

---

[37] And the idealistic youth in me loved the sage in him all the more for it.

Abu Nasr Muhammad al-Fārābī, who earned the complimentary title of "the Second Master", after Aristotle, was born around the year 870 somewhere in central Asia. We cannot be any more precise than saying that the place of his birth was a village or small town called Fārāb in that vast region. This is because the name was in use at the same time in many places there and that it is descriptive. It is the Arabised form of the Iranian compound word "par āb", because Arabic does not have the sound "p". It means an irrigated clearing, more specifically a clearing that is irrigated by a dam or elevated canal.[38] It existed in the Iranian language Soghdian, now virtually extinct in central Asia, but then a thriving tongue that had a sizeable literature, particularly in Buddhism. It lasted well into Islamic times. Similarly, although some Turkic nationalists today in such modern states as Kazakhstan, Turkmenistan and Uzbekistan claim Fārābī as one of their own ethnicity, modern scholarship is largely of the opinion that he was a Soghdian, "from the great merchant city of Fārāb, now Otrar in southern Kazakhstan".[39] An early, but sketchy, Syrian mini-biography of him says that his father was a Persian – for which read Iranian – army officer. In his own scant references to his life, he speaks only of his travelling to Damascus and Egypt in late life. He died in Damascus in December 950 or January 951, by which time Baghdad had fallen to the Iranian nationalist dynasty of the Buyids – Daylamites from the southern shores of the Caspian Sea. We

---

[38] If ever it existed in New Persian or Farsi, it has disappeared from it, but it has survived in today's Kurdish as "parow" and means irrigable. A related form, "sarow" or "sarāb, remains in common use as a place name in both Kurdish and Farsi and means "Head-of-Water" or "On-the-Water".

[39] See Christoph Baumer's *The History of Central Asia: The Age of Islam and the Mongols.* 2016, Bloomsbury, p.42.

know that he spent the bulk of his scholarly life in Baghdad before the Buyid conquest of 945. The Buyids made Baghdad their new capital but, though Shiites themselves, in expediency, preserved the Abbāsid caliph as the nominal head of Islam. Fārābī's leaving of Baghdad may have been unrelated to the upheaval, for he is recorded as having left for Syria and Egypt several years earlier.

Fārābī is often referred to as "the Father of Islamic Neo-Platonism", but this must not be taken quite at face value, for as we saw in the previous chapter, while Kindi advocated Aristotle above all other philosophers, unbeknown to himself, he was more under the influence of the Neo-Platonists in his metaphysics than he was under Aristotle's. Nevertheless, Fārābī's metaphysics is both more subtle and more secular than Kind's and in certain respects more inclined towards the Platonic original. He seems to have tried to recover the real Aristotle and the real Plato from the confusion sewn by the Translation Movement of the previous century.

Did Fārābī read enough Greek to enable him to reach Aristotle and Plato directly? I have not come across any explicit references in the sources to this important point, though scholarship on him is going through a new, active phase, aiming at collecting his works together and translating them into English. Perhaps the sources thought it unnecessary to point out the obvious. Perhaps all such masters of philosophy were expected to speak Greek as a matter of necessity. Some are known to have even read Sanskrit. But there are some indirect indications that he did read Greek. One is that his knowledge of Aristotle is vastly deeper than was Kindi's. Another pointer may be that it is hard to imagine someone who earned universal recognition among his contemporaries as "the Second Master" after Aristotle would have been given that accolade if he relied only on the translations of others for his knowledge, and possibly

119

faulty translations, too. Nor would it have been hard for him to find Greeks in Baghdad or, during his youth, in Soghdiana, who made a living out of teaching the language. Indeed, one may also expect that he also acquired a proficiency in Latin, the official language of the neighbouring Byzantines. He borrows significantly from the Roman Stoics. One further pointer may well be that his principle teacher in "the sciences of Yunān" was the Arab Christian cleric Yuhanna ibn Haylān. Fārābī also lived an unusually long life, dying at around the age of eighty. He had money, opportunity and leisure to equip himself with the tools of his trade, the main languages of the philosophy of his time and place. On the other hand, in some places his knowledge of Aristotle and Plato appears sketchy and misapprehended.[40] The reply to this latter observation may be that he would not have been alone, even in our time!

We may assume that Fārābī knew some of the well-known heretics and freethinkers of his years in Baghdad, such as his fellow Iranian Abu Bakr al-Rāzi. The circles in which such men moved were small. Is it possible that the descenters failed to affect his thinking completely? Or was it the case that he compromised his personal integrity by giving priority to the needs of his career? There has long been a debate on whether he grappled with a dilemma in this respect, and that he believed that, as in Plato's Republic, certain truths were to be held back from the ignorant masses. This is the esoteric versus the exoteric dilemma. Fārābī is certainly more secular in his ontology, the metaphysics of Existence, than was Allah-obsessed Kindi, and he does not seem keen to dwell on the need for a creator of the world. I shall return to the question later in this chapter. Let us examine the philosophy of Rāzi for a moment.

---

[40] Peter Adamson, in his Philosophy in the Islamic World, Chapter 9.

Abu Bakr Muhammad ibn Zakariyā al-Rāzi (known in the west as Rhazes) was the most notorious freethinker among Fārābī's contemporaries and hailed, as his name indicates, from the central-Iranian city of Ray. He gained fame early as a physician who dared to criticise even the great Galen, though also expressing deep admiration for that ancient doctor. So famous did Rāzī become as a clinical physician that the caliph in Baghdad commissioned him to design and build for the city "the largest bimārestān in the world". But Rāzi's outspokenness on rationality and religion became a problem and caused him to fall out of favour. Perhaps as a result of this, only his voluminous medical writings have been preserved. In a clear refutation of prophesy, he wrote that God would not favour any one individual among us with special knowledge or understanding. We were able to think for ourselves. We were rational beings. We had reason and intelligence and could distinguish right from wrong, false from true. The great Bīrūni says that he wrote two books that were deemed unacceptable. What has come down to us from his controversial opinions is what his opponents chose to relate in their critiques of him. But even though scant, these may be enough for us to make up a relatively coherent mental image of him as a thinker. Rāzi believed that reality was made of five eternal elements or principles: They were God, the soul, matter, time and place. If you can bring yourself to believe in spirits and angels, such as God and the soul, this is not quite an outdated estimation as it might seem. Matter-energy and space-time are the components of the universe in Einsteinian physics. I think that if, on this basis alone, a modern person is asked which philosopher of that age he would choose to follow, one should have no hesitation in opting for Rāzi.

The position of God in Rāzi is noteworthy. His God is similar to, but also perhaps a little more than, the artisan-manager of Aristotle and Plato. As with them, he thinks that the basics of the

121

world already existed with God at the beginning. But unlike them, he thinks that the basics were diffuse forms. There were diffuse forms of matter, time and place which God then transformed as he wished them to become. This makes God a creator, though not of an absolute type, more the kind of artist who creates an image out of pigments. As for matter, it is atomic, not as the geometric shapes that Plato envisaged in the Timaeus, but as particles moving in the void, as taught by the pre-Socratics Leucippus and Democritus. As we have lost Rāzī's philosophical writings, we must hope that he would not have been dogmatic with any of these claims. I expect that he would merely have declared a preference for the pre-Socratics. His envisaging of Time as an eternal principle may echo Zurwānism, the revering of Zurwān or Time as a deity in Sasanian Zoroastrianism, as we saw earlier. But be that as it may, overall, Rāzi's conclusions were clearly the complete opposite of the Islamic orthodoxy being imposed all around him. His denunciation of all prophets as fraudulent or delusional, in particular, would have been most uncomfortable for the great and the good of the caliphate to bear. And yet, somehow, he succeeded in dying in his own bed, though back in his birthplace of Ray, blind and isolated.

Returning to Fārābī, his views on mathematics, Aristotle's zoology and physical phenomena, such as his denial of the possibility of vacuums, or on music on which he wrote a widely influential book called The Great Book of Music[41] need not

---

[41] Kitāb al Musīqā al Kebīr, in Arabic. It is the most important book of musical theory and practice in medieval Islam, though it treats music only as a prop to the poet's work. Within only about 80 years after Fārābī's death, the Italian monk Guido of Arezzo gave the world its present system of stave notation, without which we would not today have the string quartets of Beethoven!

detain us. In any case, they were mostly mere commentaries on the ancients. But he had several areas of special interest in philosophy and metaphysics which in places go beyond enunciations of the teachers of the past. On the whole, it would be true to say that his great heroes were Aristotle and Plato, while he also exhibited the influence of the Neo-Platonists. He used the latter to minimise the differences between Plato and Aristotle, and he claimed that the two great masters could live side by side with prophethood and revelation. This is where he may be expedient, and yet not succeeding in appeasing the orthodox. He does not put the prophet of Islam on a pedestal, as they would have expected him to do, and his God is more the singular pure spirit, "The One" of the pagan Plotinus, not the judgemental patriarch of the Koran.

Fārābī's surviving works can be divided into two groups: philosophy, including logic, in one division, and the so-called mathematical sciences, including music, in the other. In the former group, he is prolific on language, logic, metaphysics and politics. A book on the Nicomachean Ethics has been lost, but Averroes and two other Andalusian philosophers in the twelfth century refer to it as having influenced them. If, in the lost book, Fārābī supported Aristotle's ethics, it must be regarded as a disappointment. Aristotle recommended, for example, harsh treatment for slaves and he envisaged no justification for permitting women any influence on the life of the polity. If this is the case, and it may not be, it would have reinforced the position of the most inflexible males of his time. Indeed, Aristotle's ethics may explain, at least partly, why he has been preferred over Plato as the philosopher most extraordinary in the world of Islam.

Fārābī is particularly emphatic on the importance of logic in human discourse, both among philosophers and ordinary people. He has a long commentary on the second segment of Aristotle's

123

Organon, the Peri Hermeneias or On Interpretation, that deals with the relationship between language and logic, as well as on the Prior Analytics or syllogistic on reasoning. The most-widely discussed part of the Organon, the Categories, also exercises him. Among these, possible subjects of human understanding, are substance, i.e. the essence of things, and time, place and contingency. Fārābī is insistent that the key to ensuring happiness in life is the possession of a logically trained mind. Logic was free of moral judgement and served all languages and cultures as an indispensable tool of clear communication. Can we see in this another hint at his not being convinced by the truth of revelations? According to Averroes, Fārābī denied that the human soul could be eternal. He also tried, wherever possible, to avoid discussing religion as a general subject, saying only that faith and organised religion were important to the masses.

In politics, Fārābī seems to have been less influenced by Aristotle than by Plato. In his curiously named book, The Opinions of the People of the Virtuous City, he recommends that the ideal state be directed by a philosopher king along the lines of The Republic, with its communistic society and liberality towards women. Some are of the belief that Fārābī inclined towards the Shiites in advocating that the leadership of the Islamic state be in the hands of descendants of the Prophet, for they would be less inclined towards meddling in the details of daily politics. Others deny the claim. One problem is that there exists no information on a chronology of his writings, except that, perhaps The Opinion was among his last works. No evolution of his thought from youth to maturity can thus be discerned.

***

To sum up Fārābī, we should perhaps begin by saying that he was a system-builder. The term is one of damnation today, but it need not always be so, in my opinion. Further, we often use the label too liberally. A bad system builder is one who, in competition with holy scripture, tries to provide ready answers to all possible questions and, in doing so, is dogmatic. He makes a single basic assumption, say on the reason for existence, and proceeds to build a mighty castle on it. In the case of Fārābī, perhaps we could be more charitable. Some modern commentators on him say that he created "a coherent body of philosophy". One is reminded of Russell, who, together with Frege, overthrew 2000 years of the domination of Aristotelian logic. In just one of his slimmest volumes entitled In Praise of Idleness, he has essays on fifteen different subjects, ranging from "useless knowledge" and "Youthful Cynicism" to "On Comets" and "What is the Soul?". Russell had roamed over too many graveyards of philosophical system builders, especially Hegel, to wish to be buried among them, but the description of creating "a coherent body of philosophy" applies equally to him. He offered his hundreds of millions of readers and admirers all over the world an almost self-sufficient philosophy of "the good life".

Fārābī was important on quite a number of fronts. He achieved a more accurate understanding of the ancients than had Kindi; he helped further to naturalise Greek philosophy in the more hostile environment of the new Islamic empires and even far beyond; and he made some important contributions of his own, including in the theory and philosophy of music which he raised to a new height of prestige[42] among Muslims. He also proved an inspiring

---

[42] Alas subsequently in the Islamic world, musicians have often been regarded as mere entertainers. Compare that to the time of the Sasanian emperor Wahrām V in Chapter IV, who elevated them to

125

exemplar to future Muslim philosophers. From his student Yahya Ibn Adī, the Arab Jacobite Christian cleric in Baghdad, to Maimonides, the greatest Jewish thinker of the Middle Ages in Cairo a couple of centuries later, every philosopher in every field could feel himself to be in his debt. He gained further influence after his death through translation into Latin. Outside philosophy, too, he was of immense value to those in society at large who looked up to their betters for intellectual enrichment. For them, he brought dignity to Islamic civilisation, for what is a civilisation without laying claim to intellectual attainment?

In the next chapter, I shall examine the life and philosophy of Avicenna, who regarded himself as following in Fārābī's steps, yet rose to overshadow him, quite unfortunately, some may think.

---

the ranks of the aristocracy. Even in Europe, that level of honour has not been breached. Beethoven, arguably one of the greatest men who have ever lived, was prevented from marrying the daughter of an even minor nobleman.

EIGHT

Avicenna the Persian

Never of teachers did I go deprived.
Then more theorem I myself contrived.
Seventy-two years, day and night, I thought:
Only to conclude that I knew naught![44]

If you read the opening paragraph of the 9,000-word entry on
Avicenna in the great Stanford Encyclopedia of Philosophy, you
might think that a quack doctor was being summed up, a man

---

[43] Avicenna's great Canon of Medicine was translated into Latin as
early as the twelfth century and was taught at most European
universities until relatively recent times. This printed copy dates to
1484 and is on display in the P. I. Nixon Medical History Library
in San Antonio, Texas.

[44] Omar Khayyām, a couple of generations after Avicenna. My
translation. See Chapter 10.

who had a ready answer to every question that anyone might ask of him, not a man whose intellect you would respect. Here it is:

> In his work he combined the disparate strands of philosophical/scientific thinking in Greek late antiquity and early Islam into a rationally rigorous and self-consistent scientific system that encompassed and explained all reality, including the tenets of revealed religion and its theological and mystical elaborations. ...

Is this merely thoughtless writing? "A rationally rigorous and self-consistent scientific system that encompassed and *explained all reality,* including the tenets of revealed religion and its theological and mystical elaborations"! The italics are mine.

Surely the man who became one of the most influential thinkers of his time and for many centuries after his time, both in the vast world of Islam and in the equally vast world of Latin Christendom, could not be this bad as a thinker: someone who would claim, with iron confidence, that he had proved that science and mysticism did not contradict one another, a philosopher who was so utterly un-Socratic, so utterly without humility, as to claim that he had explained all reality for the first time in history? Surely this cannot be the real view of the writer of the entry?

I have not had the pleasure of meeting the renowned Dimitri Gutas, Emeritus Professor of Arabic and Islamic philosophy at Yale University, though we are both ancient men and I have met many such men. But I wonder: If I could ask which trait he would choose, the Socratic doubt and humility of an Omar Khayyām as quoted above, or the claims of anyone who said he had combined science and mysticism, what would his answer be? Surely you would expect of him to say that, in the end, the navel-gazing that largely produced the metaphysics of the ancients proved a dead end, that it did not improve the wisdom or knowledge of their hapless readers and, in many cases, even

128

misled them into falsehood. In that case, why praise such confidence tricksters sky high?

There may be a number of explanations for this class of writing in histories of philosophy. One may be the usual inclination of busy editors to commission the last "expert" who had published a book on the subject, for example a biographer of Ghazālī, without asking whether he might have been funded by, say, the sheikhs of Dubai. Another may well be the plaudible desire of well-meaning Western intellectuals to be generous towards "the other", and a third the so-called "biographer's syndrome", that afflicts someone who has spent years immersed in the minutiae of a last life and grown to identify with him. I have myself suffered from it.

This is not, at all, to say that denouncing the thinkers of the past for their now-antiquated beliefs, let alone their scientific ignorance compared to modern people, has a place in histories of philosophy, as opposed to polemical works that set out to repudiate them. But going to the other extreme is surely equally wrong. Nor is heaping intellectual kudos on the heads of the religious fanatics of the past harmless, if Avicenna was indeed a religious fanatic, which must be doubted in view of the autobiography which he has left us (See the appendix). Praising any such fanatics is a gift to today's oppressive theocrats in such afflicted lands as the Islamic Republic of Iran or the Islamic Emirate of Afghanistan. We can be certain that the Stanford article has been translated into a dozen languages in the Islamic world and that the translators have been rewarded handsomely from the taxes of the poor.

I cannot, of course, believe that Professor Gutas believes what he has written, that science and mysticism were successfully reconciled by Avicenna. But he ought to have made it clear that he believes it was Avicenna who believed that he had succeeded

129

in doing so. The venerable professor also knows that Avicenna was no innocent pioneer isolated from the rest of humanity, completely unaware that in his own time and region he was being denounced by his equals for his writings. The Syrian poet and philosopher Abul Alā al Ma'arri was one such famous voice, and so was Avicenna's fellow Persian philosopher Suhravardi who was executed for rejecting Islam wholesale. Let me quote Khayyām again, a man who studied under a student of Avicenna's and admired his medicine. In the following quatrain, which I believe I have succeeded in translating almost verbatim, Khayyām invokes the famous humility of Socrates to puncture the fake profundities of those who pretended complete certainty about the nature of reality:

This Sea of Being has come out of naught.
No glimpse of its truth has anyone caught.
Many a clown has put forth his thought:
From the Other Side, News cannot be sought!

Inserting a few words about the existence of those other voices into the introductory assessment of Avicenna would have improved the professor's otherwise admirable article.

Avicenna, as just mentioned, is still widely read by Muslims and often referred to in reverential terms by them. He was also, as again mentioned, a philosopher who influenced the writings of myriad others who came after him, in both the rival worlds of Islam and Christianity. Despite his obnoxious character, he must be included in any history of philosophy such as this account.

The precise year of birth of Abu Ali al-Husayn ibn Abdallah ibn Sina is not known. But from a careful reading of the autobiography it would seem that it was somewhere in the middle or late 970s. He was born in the rather civilised city of Bukhārā in central Asia, a city which had recently patronised a new flowering of Persian literature under a dynasty called the

130

Sāmānids. Under these monarchs, a large region of the Iranian world, Greater Khorāsān, had re-discovered its rich pre-Islamic past and had revived the Persian language as a medium of poetry and history against the wishes of Muslim fundamentalists who wished the tongue extinguished and replaced by Arabic. Further, while the Sāmānids were themselves Sunni Muslims, they tolerated other creeds, such as Ismā'ili Shiites to whom Avicenna's family belonged, or the Jews, Christians and Zoroastrians. Indeed, one of their poets, Daqīqī, had gained widespread plaudit for writing this blasphemous quatrain:

Four blessings above all has Daqīqī chosen
In this battleground of beauty and repellence:
The ruby of lips, the cry of the harp,
The taste of old wine, and the creed of Zarathustra!

By the age of seventeen years and six months, Avicenna says, he was so well read in medicine and so practiced in it that his fame as a doctor had spread far and wide, to the extent that the king in Bukhārā asked him to join the team of doctors who were treating him for an acute abdominal pain. The king was impressed and allowed him access to his private library, where the young man found books on philosophy, mathematics, astronomy and literature that he "had not even suspected existing".[45] They were largely translations from Greek into Arabic, as we saw in the

---

[45] The attached biography and its supplement by one of his students is only about 4700 words long, but apart from the light it casts on his life and works and rather shameful character, it also gives a lively impression of Iranian society and politics in a time of exceptional turmoil under the Sāmānid and Buyid dynasties in the first half of the eleventh century.

previous two chapters, and thus Avicenna acquired a solid grounding in the knowledge of the ancient masters early in life.

Unfortunately for him, the Sāmānids fell in 999 to Turkish invaders, the Qarakhānids, from the interior of central Asia, and these had only recently converted to Islam and were, at first, specially intolerant of Shiites. This forced Avicenna to flee for central Iran. There, the rulers, the Būyids, were fellow Shiites and hailed from the region of Daylam on the southern shores of the Caspian Sea. Their homeland had never been conquered by Arab Muslims. As a result, they, too, as with the Sāmānids of Bukhārā and Samarkand, were proud of their Zoroastrian past. They had recently captured Baghdad, but, out of expediency, had allowed the Abbāsid caliphs there to continue functioning as the spiritual heads of Sunni Islam, without permitting them any real political or military power..

Beginning in the city of Ray, whose ruins are near today's Tehran, Avicenna lived a semi-nomadic life, seeking refuge at the door of one prince after another, but he was fortunate. Everywhere, it seems, his fame as a physician had travelled before him, and if there is only one kind of expert whom rulers forgive for almost any crime, it is a physician who promises them a long life. This is not to say that the rulers in his case did not find pride in giving shelter to philosophers whose profound words they did not understand. On the contrary and often, when they were strong enough not to need the approval of their clerics, the Buyids conferred honours and riches on such men as Avicenna, as they did their bards to immortalise their power and glory. Avicenna benefited from such weaknesses.

Beside his unbecoming lust for women and money, Avicenna also craved high administrative office for the power of patronage that it offered him. As his adoring student and assistant says, teaching philosophy and writing books – though both were themselves also lucrative preoccupations – were distractions to him from the concerns of the day as grand vizier, to be performed chiefly in the evenings, over wine and dinner. He also earned large fees from treating rich patients. He was vain, avaricious, proud and vengeful. He had a large chunk of Wagner in him without the charms of that artist![46]

Let us examine his main works, especially those that affected the thinking of later writers, both in the Islamic world and in Europe, while asking also if he made any useful contributions to philosophy.

Avicenna was a prolific writer, largely, one feels, because there was a constant and lucrative demand on him by princes and rich sponsors, and he designed his products to order. His two earliest commissions, which were compendiums or summae of all the parts of philosophy as delineated by Aristotle and the Alexandrians, have been lost, but they are really no loss! He repeated his earlier writings habitually as he received new commissions and, in any case, it is his later, mature works that ought to interest us. If we ignore his huge tome on medicine, The Canon, for the moment, two other categories of his works need consideration. They are his encyclopaedic, twenty-five-volume summa of philosophy, The Healing, with its misleading title, which means healing from ignorance, not from illnesses, and his more scattered commentaries on religion, specifically Islam, some would say too specifically.

---

[46] Roger Scruton, who puzzled me with his love of Wagner's music, was fond of saying that Avicenna was the only philosopher known to him "who died from drinking and shagging". I would not say so. He died from an unrelated illness treated badly by himself, the doctor who caused his own death! See the end of the Appendix.

The Kitāb ash-Shifā' or The Book of Healing has four parts: logic, the natural sciences, mathematics (including Ptolemaic astronomy), and metaphysics, Ilāhiyāt in Arabic, which really means the knowledge of God only.

The style is lumbering and braggart, referring to himself everywhere as "we", but if "we" is replaced with "I", it become more tolerable. As we might expect, the whole is based heavily on Aristotle, but it borrows also from the Stoics and the Neo-Platonists, and from previous Muslim writers such as Kindi and Fārābī, as well as his Khwārazmian contemporary, Bīrūnī, "the first palaeontologist". Reading the Shifā', one senses a modern scientist trying to emerge from the undergrowth covering the swamp. The writer has been observing nature and human beings minutely and has become a good psychologist as a result of many years working as a physician. For example, he knows of the effects of hypnosis on people and he is fascinated by fossils. But he cannot resist making pompous statements that are outlandish guesswork. On fossilised remains of ancient animals and plants, for example, he says that they are petrified fluids caused by a mineralising and petrifying "virtue" that emanates from the earth in stony grounds during earthquakes and landslips.

As with previous philosophers going back all the way to Aristotle, Avicenna laid great weight by logic, but he tweaked Aristotle's system to come up with his own version that subsequently dominated Muslim philosophers for some time and even influenced such Christian medieval philosophers as Albertus Magnus and William of Ockham. He invoked inductive logic such as the methods of agreement, difference and concomitant variation – variation in an attribute than can help an observer to discover its effect – which feature in the scientific method. He also developed the theory of modal logic, eventually to become his "temporally modalised" syllogistic to represent propositions that involve time, possibility and necessity.

134

In the eyes of Muslims, Avicenna succeeded in combining Aristotelianism with Neo-Platonism and a purportedly rationalistic appraisal of the Koran, the so-called science of Kalām, and he followed Fārābī in deepening the gap between "essence" and existence, essence being a set of attributes without which a being cannot be what it is, while existence is the realm of the contingent and accidental. He taught that the existence of a being cannot be deduced from the essence of that being and that contingent existents cannot exist on their own. They must ultimately end in a necessary being, a First Cause-without-a-Cause, which is God. His proposed method for proving the existence of God is subsequently both ontological and cosmological.

I said earlier that in Avicenna we sense a modern scientist struggling to emerge from the dark. In his philosophy of science, he criticises Aristotelian induction because, he says, it cannot result in certainty regarding realities. He lays more emphasis on experimentation and demonstration, foreshadowing Bacon.[47]

In the matter of religion, Avicenna took a step backwards. Instead of following Fārābī in treating it as a phenomenon, he concentrated his attention on one specific creed, Islam. This laid him open to severe criticism by his contemporaries for not being a philosopher, but a mere theologian. He was, of course, a statesman constantly in the public eye and knowing that his paymasters were wary of associating with someone in the highest ranks of their government who was not religiously respectable. But I think that he did not need to be in government service and he did not need, even as a statesman, to go to the

---

[47] In December 1131, the family of Omar Khayyām reported that it was this book that he was reading when he died at the age of 83. See Teimourian in the Bibliography.

lengths that he did to please his sponsoring kings and princes. With regard to the specific religion of the state, he could have been less adulatory, more of an objective observer, as his successor in distant Andalusia would in particular choose to be a century later. Indeed Averroes lived under a hostile, a censorious government. Instead, Avicenna devoted many books to trying to prove the truth of such doctrines as the immortality of the soul and the resurrection of the body in a physical heaven complete with its former soul. He felt that he had to write even on the efficacy of prayer. Predictably, an anti-Avicennan movement came into being among educated Muslims who accused him of making too many concessions to the orthodox, even if he sometimes resorted to oblique and mystical language. This pandering to the mob may well be one of the explanations of his continued popularity in later times among Muslims.

Finally a brief description of his most famous book, Al-Qānūn fil-Tibb, the Canon of Medicine, may be apt here, for two reasons: First, that in those times, the present distinction between philosophy and the sciences did not exist, and, second, that a quote from it can illustrate his cumbrous language. The Canon runs to five volumes and achieved such renown that, for centuries afterwards, it remained the main book of reference for physicians both in the Middle East and in Europe. It is based on Galen and Hippocrates and Avicenna adapts it to Aristotle's natural philosophy, with concessions made to Persian culture and Islamic doctrine. The infamous four humours of ancient medicine are its underpinning pillars. The following quotation, almighty nonsense, is from its section on pulse:

> Through combining the four humours in different proportions, the Almighty created the organs. So, muscles have more blood, bone has more black bile, the brain has a preponderance of phlegm and the lungs more yellow bile. ... The Almighty made the soul from

136

the softness of the humours, with each soul having its own weight.
… The soul lives in the heart and the arteries.[48]

The Canon is sometimes described as the most famous text book of medicine ever written. It was only deposed from the pedestal by better-informed Renaissance professionals, but by then it had probably killed more people than it had saved, its most famous victim being the doctor himself!

Avicenna is also prolific in his other "scientific" writings, almost all of them based ultimately on Aristotle, Ptolemy and the like, while also containing some fine-tunings by Avicenna. They range from meteorology and astronomy to alchemy and the classification of animals.

***

Avicenna overshadowed Fārābī, the Islamic philosophical star of the previous century, as the latter had put his own predecessor Kindi in the shade. Fārābī seems to me the deeper and more honest thinker of the three, for he chose to avoid discussing religion, wherever he could, describing it as what the masses needed and stressing its interest as a social phenomenon to philosophers.

In the end, all these thinkers are important in the sense that they enhanced the reputational standing of Greek reasoning in the Islamic world, to the extent that, for example, when Ghazālī launched his famous attack on the philosophers (see Chapter 10), he had to confess that Greek philosophy, as expounded especially by Avicenna, was still the best path to truth.

In the next chapter, I shall examine the last great philosopher of the Muslim world, Averroes. Did he similarly overshadow all

---

[48] My translation.

his predecessors? Somehow I expect to find that the answer is both yes and no.

NINE

Averroes the Berber

There is absolutely no reason to judge the fact that he was, in the depths of his being, what we call a freethinker, and that he must have had to mask carefully his most intimate convictions in order to escape the threats of a politically powerful religious orthodoxy.[50]

Unlike Avicenna who died the chief minister of a state, Averroes suffered isolation and disgrace. We may choose not to read much

---

[49] "The Triumph of Thomas Aquinas Over Averroes" by the Florentine painter of the fifteenth century Benozzo Gozzoli, showing how intermingled Christian and Muslim thought had become as a result of Averroes's writings in late medieval times.

[50] Roger Arnaldez in *Averroes: A Rationalist in Islam,* p119. See the Bibliography.

into this contrast, for Averroes lived in the hostile environment of a newly-established, proselytising theocracy. For a better parallel, we may have to go back a century earlier to the great Rāzī, who also suffered isolation and disgrace when the Abbāsids still wielded real power. Even then, we cannot be too confident. The lines have grown faint. Not many facts have survived of the intimate circumstances of either life, that of Averroes and that of Rāzī. But it is noteworthy that they lived under monarchies that derived their legitimacy from pretending to deputise for Allah on Earth, the Al-Mohads in Marrakesh and the Abbāsids in Baghdad. Also, Averroes was never as outspoken as Rāzī had been. As far as we know, he never denounced prophets as frauds. He merely placed religion and philosophy into different categories. The dangers to his liberty seem to have arisen from his ideas about what made a state morally legitimate. His ideal contrasted sharply from the reality of the Al-Mohads' harsh governance. They had honoured him as their chief physician and Islamic judge, but his late-life advocacy that the law must be compatible with natural justice and evolve with the needs of society had spread too far. He was being read from Rome to Cairo to Baghdad to Samarkand. Despite his life-long service to the Al-Mohads, he could no-longer be tolerated, for in a time of uncertainty, when Andalusia was being threatened by a resurgent Christianity in the north, the support of the orthodox clergy had become the more urgent need. Some of the clergy claimed that Averroes preferred the Greeks and Romans to Islam. This was probably true. He wanted women to have the possibility of becoming rulers.

Abul-Walīd Muhammad ibn Ahmad ibn Rushd (1126-98) was born and brought up in Cordoba. At the time, Andalusia was a province of the North-African Berber empire of the Morāvids.[51] His family enjoyed high religious and intellectual standing in the region, with his father and grandfather both being front-ranking Islamic judges. But in 1146, when he was 20 years old, a new Muslim cult led by a man who claimed to be the Mahdi, the Savour, overthrew the Morāvids. Averroes could not have been pleased, but there was no alternative to bowing to power. As a result, he was allowed to function in the steps of his forebears. In 1169 in Marrakesh, when he was 42 years old, he was introduced to a new caliph and was surprised by the ruler's interest in philosophy. He was commissioned to write an accessible introduction to Aristotle and thus began in earnest his career as a commentator on Greek thought.

Averroes was promoted to be chief Islamic judge in both Seville and Cordoba, as well as being appointed the caliph's personal physician in Marrakesh. Despite these obligations, he wrote prolifically on philosophy and his fame as a thinker overshadowed his expertise as doctor and judge. In 1195, three years before his death, however, he was tried for heresy and his books were ordered to be burned. His life was spared, but he was exiled to the countryside of Cordoba. Towards the very end, in 1197, he was back in favour in Marrakesh. The reason has not come down to us, but it may well have been due to the personal regard of a new caliph. He died the following year.

Averroes wrote on more philosophical, medical and scientific topics than any of his Muslim predecessors, and he lived to a relatively long age of almost seventy-three years. Modern scholars attribute over one hundred substantial books and monographs to him, but the book burnings and the ostracization had their effect and some of his main works in Arabic have

---

[51] Al-Murābitūn in Arabic, meaning "those who link and unite".

disappeared. Not all, though, were lost. Translations of some of them into Latin and Hebrew have survived and this may well explain why, in the end, he proved much more influential in the non-Muslims west than he did among his fellow Muslims. I shall return to this point later.

For a review of his work, I suggest that we begin with those fields that mattered most to himself, subjects for which he risked his social standing, prosperity and even liberty, and it is precisely in those subjects that he may be said to have made real contributions to philosophy, rather than merely those works in which he expanded or commented on the metaphysical sandcastles of his inheritance from Avicenna and ultimately the Neo-Platonists and Aristotle.

As might be expected of a lawyer, justice and politics clearly motivated Averroes more than any other field of philosophy, and this may enable us to say that he was perhaps the most sincere and the most serious of the Muslim philosophers examined in this account so far. In this, as already seen, he was the opposite of Avicenna, a claim on my part which may be corroborated in his own scathing criticism of Avicenna. For the Persian grand vizier, philosophy had been a secondary activity and a distraction. By contrast, Averroes saw and cared that philosophy had social consequences, and he wanted passionately that any philosophy propounded by him affect society for the better.

He says that he wrote his Epitome on Plato's Republic because Aristotle's Politics was not available to him "as yet". In fact, the book had not been translated into Arabic. His commentary was subsequently lost, in Arabic, most probably among the books that were burned, but a translation into Hebrew is extant and, though its manuscripts are in various degrees of decay and completeness, it offers us enough to surprise us. We can perhaps even describe it as evolutionary. He rejoices in Plato's

142

communism and he applauds Plato's recommendation that women be allowed into the councils of guardians of a state. The latter would have been discovered immediately as a clear refutation of the Koranic sūra, the Nisā', devoted to the treatment of women, and it is almost certainly one reason why he was tried as a heretic. Experts tell us that the Epitome was one of his last works, and it is easy to see why he turned to it in late life. Being a good man and having, throughout a long legal career, seen too many cases of injustice against divorced and discarded women and young mothers in his own courts, Averroes as an old man decided to throw caution to the wind in the hope of making a difference. We know that, even previously, some of his legal judgements had caused him enemies among the orthodox. These would not have been slow in bringing his heretical last writings to the attention of the literalist al-Mohads.

Averroes's theology is similarly brave. While not original, and while trying to prove – again what a futile pursuit, as in the case of Kindi, Fārābī and Avicenna – that reason and revelation can be reconciled, his God stands at a great distance from the supreme deity of the Abrahamic religions. For him, God still does have the attributes of a person, but he resembles the artisan-manager of Plato and Aristotle, a being who co-exists with the world and has shaped it to his desire out of primordial, formless substance. Averroes further offends the literalists by saying that whenever a statement or command in the Koran seems to contradict common sense, it must be regarded as allegorical and needs to be interpreted in a manner that makes it acceptable.

While Averroes disagrees with some contemporary claims to prove the existence of God, such as Avicenna's necessary being, he proposes his own preferred way. He says that the existence of a creator of the world can be proved by resorting to our observance of design and providence in nature. Many entities are so intricate that they can have been designed only by an

143

intelligent being, and since the whole of the universe functions as if it is meant to nurture life, God has to be good. All of God's supposed attributes he then derives from His agency and goodness. God could not have achieved what he has without being able to see and hear, etc.

Averroes's attitude towards revelation is pragmatic and may be less sincere. The masses are incapable of understanding complicated concepts. They need the explanation of the world, as well as their codes of conduct towards one another, to be readily imaginable as sensible. Thus they need anthropomorphic stories of creation, heaven and hell, as conveyed in holy books. They sometimes also need to be coerced to obey their betters, though persuasion is a better policy. For the educated elite, however, philosophy is a necessity. They can arrive at the truths of religion through reason. These thoughts were formulated in his middle years, when he was still keen to retain his official positions.

Averroes's many publications on medicine, astronomy, natural philosophy and the like need not divert us here, but he is well known for a book that he wrote to repudiate Ghazālī, the Persian Ash'arite firebrand who had died in 1111, a decade or so before his birth. In response to Ghazālī's chosen title for his book, The Incoherence of the Philosophers (Tahāfut al-Falāsifah), Averroes chose his to be The Incoherence of The Incoherence. Ghazālī's main target of attack had been Muslim philosophers as exemplified by Avicenna, with their borrowings from the Neo-Platonists and the Greek masters. In his response, Averroes defends philosophers in general, especially Aristotelians, but sometimes he sides with Ghazālī against Avicenna. I shall turn to Ghazālī in greater detail in the next chapter, where I will examine the beginnings of the plight of philosophy among Muslims. For the time being, I will examine the extent of Averroes's huge posthumous influence among the Jews and

Christians of Europe and North Africa while he was almost forgotten among his fellow Muslims.

As can be seen at the start of this chapter, over two centuries after Averroes's death, a painter in Florence felt it a necessary task to show his fellow Christians that their St Aquinas had trounced the views of Averroes the Muslim. Perhaps no other image makes so clear how intermingled Muslim and Christian philosophies had become by then, early fifteenth century. What might explain this phenomenon? Why did many Christian leaders, who were strongly opposed to Islam, find it irresistible to adopt Averroes almost as one of their own?

The answer must be sought in the common human need for self-respect, our preference to think for ourselves, rather than put our trust wholly in authority. The medieval Church, which had acquired widespread repute as corrupt, demanded unflinching obedience to its interpretations of Christian doctrines, but some of its monks and priests found the thinking of the infidel more convincing and more humane. As Aristotle had said so famously, humans, by nature, wanted to know, and it helped that the infidel in question here said he was devoted to Aristotle.

It seems that the Jews, who were more familiar with the Arabic language due to their having communities on both sides of the divide and traversed the borders more frequently, played an important part in taking Averroes's ideas into the interior of Europe. They translated virtually all of his major works into Hebrew and there were often line-by-line commentaries on Aristotle, which Averroes was trying to disentangle from the Neo-Platonist infestation caused by the Abbāsid Translation Movement. Many of the Hebrew translations were subsequently turned into Latin and consulted widely, to the extent that Averroes came to be known in Europe simply as "the commentator". Some even came to view him as the greater master, putting Aristotle in the shade. In North Africa, too, it is on record that when the Jewish philosopher Maimonides received a batch of Averroes's works, he praised the master exuberantly, saying that he agreed with him in all respects.

Unfortunately, Averroes the reporter is frequently an undisciplined reporter. He inserts his own opinions into his commentary without always distinguishing himself from Aristotle or – in the case of the Republic – Plato. When the original Greek source or its Latin translation has been lost, a considerable problem arises for historians of philosophy.

Thus partially flawed, Averroes quicky found a foothold in such Christian centres of learning as the University of Paris and his influence grew rapidly at a time when new universities were being set up in many places in north-western Europe. And so came into being a new school of thought called Averroism. The term appears first in the writings of Aquinos. He called one of his polemics De Unitate Intellectus Contra Averroistas, Against the Averroists' Unicity of the Intellect. But the label may well have been in use in Christian circles previously. Aquinas stopped writing in 1277. That is barely half-a-century after Averroes's death in 1198, and the fact that Aquinas felt so alarmed, so compelled, as to need to write a book of advocacy against what he called "the path to unbelief" is telling. Averroes, a Muslim enemy, had become a prestigious thinker among Christians, and so early.

Why? What were those of his thoughts that appealed strongly to the monks and priests of Catholic Europe?

Whether or not Averroes would have agreed with the interpretations that the Europeans put on his advocacies is another matter. Philosophers are frequently misunderstood, even by their own students. An example of this in his case may be that among his new supporters, such commentators as Siger of

146

Brabant and Boetius of Dacia said that he believed in two kinds of truth: One to be attained through the study of scripture, the other through science. This is doubtful, though it cannot be ruled out, given the fact that Averroes lived under a censorious fundamentalist caliphate and could not always speak clearly. It is generally believed now that he thought otherwise, that truth was one and the same, but could be reached in two different ways. One of these was prophetic revelation, the other Aristotelian science. But as we have also seen, he advocated that if prophetic scripture did not appear to make sense, it had been meant not to be taken at face value, that it was allegorical and should therefore be interpreted in a matter that made it sensible. In other words, reason was superior to faith.

The timing of Europe's reception of Averroes may be a relevant factor. The middle years of the thirteenth century saw the first stirrings of the movement that later came to be known as the Renaissance. The continent's population was growing, new towns were being founded in all directions and an expanding merchant class longed for intellectual self-respect and self-improvement and began to look on the ancient Greeks and Romans with new admiration. The European Averroists thus found it helpful that Averroes portrayed himself as an unyielding devotee of Aristotle and Plato, the two founding fathers of European thought. Indeed, the Averroists also became known as The Radical Aristotelians.

Despite widespread criticism by conservative Christian theologians, such as in the Condemnations of 1210-1277 by Bishop Etienne Tempier of Paris, bastions of Averroism thrived in such centres of learning as Padua, with one famous martyr to the cause of Averroism being as late as 1600 in the shape of Giordano Bruno who was burnt at the stake in Rome. The indictment against him cited especially his refutations of Christ's virgin birth, eternal damnation, the Trinity, transubstantiation,

147

etc, all of which doctrines Averroes would have found contrary to reason and therefore unacceptable.

It is interesting also that the Condemnations of 1210-77 in many places repeated the objections levied against philosophers by the Sunni firebrand of Nishāpūr, of whom more in the next chapter.

***

To sum up, let us return to the question I asked at the end of the previous chapter. Did Averroes overshadow his predecessor Avicenna? The answer has to be both yes and no. He did overshadow Avicenna resoundingly in the Christian and Jewish West, but failed completely among his fellow Muslims in the East. Whereas, as we have just seen, he became so revered in European intellectual circles as to cause a rift in the Church, in the Muslim world he quickly and irreversibly became merely a figure of curiosity. For me, there is no comparison. He was the most able thinker of all the front-ranking philosophers of Islam, for his appeal to reason, combined with his deep sympathy for fragile human beings and his understanding of the vulnerabilities of untrained masses to superstition, can still be defended in our time.[52]

---

[52] See my own effort in that direction in The Ultimate Question: in search of God in a godless universe, London, 2024.

TEN
Philosophy takes Flight: Ghazāli v. Khayyām

Iran's ruling Shiites have not forgiven Ghazālī for backing the wrong side! In the desert in Khorāsān is his bus-stop shelter of a mausoleum, a tin roof on iron poles.

In old Mesopotamia lived a pious Jew called Isac. Everyone loved him. One day, he found himself in the middle of a flood. It was not unusual. In Mesopotamia, Jews and floods were famous together. So he was not worried. His ancestors had survived worse. As a result, when the waters were only knee-high and a group of neighbours arrived with a boat and urged him to climb on broad, he refused. They insisted. "There's no point, Uncle Isac", they said. "Your bed and rugs and washing machine are already ruined". He told them: "Thank you very much, but God will not let me down". The neighbours, not

149

blessed by faith, shook their heads and left. The waters kept rising and Isac was forced to climb to the roof of his hut. Then a young boy-scout arrived in a kayak. "Uncle Isac", he shouted. "Don't worry about the size of this little thing. It can take the weight of both of us". Isac smiled serenely and thanked the boy. "Don't worry, my dear son. God will find a way". The waters continued to rise and reached his chest. He was about to be swept away, when, suddenly, out of the blue, a helicopter appeared and threw a rope onto the water. The pilots gesticulated to Isac to grasp it. But Isac's faith held steadfast. He gesticulated back: "No, thank you". The helicopter flew away in disbelief and poor Isac drowned, only to wake up in Heaven. But instead of being happy, he was angry. He asked the stewardesses to take him to God straight away and they did. When God opened the door, Isac shouted at Him. "What happened to you", he asked? "Am I not one of your chosen people?" God was not pleased. He rolled his eyes to the High Heavens and sighed. "My God!", He shouted. "Didn't I send you two boats and a helicopter?".[53]

Isac was stunned. God's love and care left him speechless, at which point God came back. "I'll tell you another thing. I don't have any helicopters of my own. I had to go to the Devil to hire one and you can guess how much he charged me".

When Isac had recovered, he apologised to God and accepted the generous freehold of a great mansion nearby. In the evening, angels served him a sumptuous meal of rare meats and old wines, and a quarter played for him one of his favourite string quartets by Beethoven, when, suddenly, a shattering thought occurred to him. "Wait a minute", he said to himself. "We Jews boast that

---

[53] I think that, to this point, I read this joke in one of Peter Adamson's books. The rest is my own embellishment, for which I apologise to whoever it was who made up the original, perhaps centuries ago.

our God is omnipotent. But what kind of a God is it who has to ask the Devil for a helicopter? Even Saddam had them."

The Jews – if that broad category is meaningful at all – are lucky in being able readily to ridicule themselves and this joke, without the helicopter, is only one among tens of thousands that have over many ages of calamity helped to sustain them. I think that this particular one must have been aimed at the over-zealous among them. Two sets of neighbours offered Isac the chance to save himself, but each time he stuck to an absolute faith in the intervention of an all-powerful and all-good God. He paid the price for not allowing himself even the thinnest slither of doubt.

Questioning the gods, even blaspheming against them, is as old as the birth of the Mind itself in the earliest of our species. It must surely go back to the first hunter-gatherers. In the case of Islam, it goes back to the time of Muhammed himself. There are hadiths that relate how quite a number of people in Mecca ridiculed him for claiming that he had been chosen to be God's last messenger to humanity. Such murmurs did not die out even among important figures who were among the first Muslims. Muāwiyah, the fifth caliph, is suspected of having been one such man. He was a tribal chief who smelt a winning side and joined it. When he had established himself in the grand city of Damascus as the new supreme leader and set up a new hereditary monarchy, he reverted back to his bad old ways.

Disagreements were not new. Almost immediately after Muhammed's death, some believers shouted betrayal over the interpretations that others placed on their new common faith, with one movement becoming known as the Atharists, "athar" being the Arabic word for trace or remnant. The Atharists stressed the need of the new Muslim community to preserve unity through tracing solutions to their disagreements in the guidelines of the Koran and the hadith. They insisted on needing

151

to abide by every Koranic statement or command at face value. It was dangerous to interpret those guideline according to your own tastes or temperaments. That way lay the path to discord.

Atharism's most prominent proponent at its beginning under the second caliph was a jurist in the city of Kūfa by the name of Āmir al-Kūfi al-Sha'bi, who denounced Shiites as "vultures and donkeys". His followers were equally stern and unable to allow for the compromises that any political body has to make. As a result, they never gained governmental power, even under the first Abbāsids in the next century who were picked for their strict religiosity to replace the Umayyads.

The Abbāsids, in their turn, softened and acquired imperial decadence. They began to enjoy wallowing in luxuries extracted through taxes imposed on near-destitute peasants inside the empire and raiding hapless frontier peoples for loot and slaves. They also surrounded themselves with poets and idlers who sometimes grew into "philosophers", people who asked awkward and alien questions. Some of these philosophers then organised themselves into a movement they called the Mu'tazilites, meaning they had "withdrawn" from the tiresome dispute between Sunnis and Shiites over the right succession to the prophet. Later still, they had so much idle time on their hands that they began even more awkward and foreign questions. They asked themselves, for example, if Time was as old as God, whether it already existed when God created the world? And on the basis of what knowledge did God create the world? In other words, was the Koran, God's knowledge, with him at the start already, or whether He created it? They concluded that, obviously, He created the Koran, because it spoke of the prophet and Mecca and other recent events and places. But if so, if the Koran was created in Time, it would surely date in time. It would become old-fashioned. Should its commands be obeyed still if they do not seem right or sensible?

152

The Mu'tazilites, as we saw above, gained governmental power under the freethinking caliph Ma'mūn – "the Persian boy" – and persecuted anyone who disagreed with them, often harshly so. Then their sway came to an end under caliph Mutawakkil, who fell under the spell of the opposite camp, in particular a school of literalists called the Ash'arites. The founder of the Ash'arite school of thought, a man called Abul Hasan al-Ash'ari, was a man of Kufa who had been educated as a Mu'tazilite. But when he was around the age of 40, he announced that the prophet had appeared to him three times during the fasting month of Ramadan to give him new guidelines. He had been ordered to obey only the commandments of the Koran as clearly set out in the holy book and also to follow the hadith, what the prophet had said or done, while, also, at the same time, retaining the Mu'tazilite method of reasoning for a better understanding of Islamic theology. Thus al-Ash'ari began to oppose the idea that the Koran had been created in time, and he stressed the eternity of God's attributes. God could see, hear and speak, he said. He had intelligence and agency. Al-Ash'ari combined, too, the validity of both predestination and free will. In some other respects, however, he struck his contemporaries as a moderate. He preached that if a Muslim committed some crimes, such as drinking and thieving, he should not be denounced as an apostate and expelled from the faith. He should be given the chance to repent and repair himself. Similarly, against the violent practices of an earlier movement of rebels, the Khārijites, who had assassinated the fourth caliph Ali for allegedly not being severe enough against Umayyads, he denounced any contemplation of assassinating a ruler for un-Islamic behaviour. Nevertheless, in step with other literalists, he denounced Shiites as heretics. By striking upon this so-called "middle way", Ash'arism has continued in force to the present age, becoming the dominant school of theology in Sunni Islam. In the late eleventh century, it bred one particularly influential figure, Abū Hāmid al-Ghazālī at-Tūsi.

Ghazālī was a conflicted personality who was given into histrionics, visions and spiritual crises. Nevertheless, such has been his influence down the centuries that some commentators describe him as the man who closed the door to the progress of philosophy and science in the world of Islam. As I hinted earlier, he also wielded a strong influence over Christian theorists, such as Aquinas, known among them as Algazelus. Some of his modern Sunni adulators believe him to have been predicted by the prophet himself as a Mujaddid. He and his kind appear among Muslims once every hundred years to restore their faith in Islam.

Be that as it may, Algazelus was, from the beginning, not every Muslim's model of a godly man. One damnatory story has him in the presence of his former teacher Omar Khayyām at a gathering of the great and good of Isfahān, when he suddenly decides to humiliate Khayyām. He asks the empire's leading astronomer why philosophers have chosen two points at the two extremities of the Earth as its poles when those two points are no different from any other points? Khayyām begins to answer and the answer turns out not to be brief, because he suspects that Ghazālī intends to use what he says to denounce him as a heretic. As Khayyām is still speaking, the voice of the mu'azzin is heard from a nearby mosque and Ghazālī rises to leave, shouting "The truth has arrived and falsehood is put to flight". At the time, Ghazālī enjoyed the strong support of the grand vizier and knew that he, the grand vizier, had come to dislike Khayyām for his freethinking and his influence over the Shah. The story went "viral", as we would say today, and both Grand Vizier Nizām al-Mulk and the Shah would have heard it, as was probably Ghazālī's precise intention. I do not know what Khayyām's answer was, but he could have merely mentioned that Ghazālī need only hang a piece of lodestone by a sting in the air. Lodestones had been in use for millennia as an aid to navigation. Hung by a sting, they align themselves north-south, along the line of the two magnetic poles. Khayyām would have been familiar with the effect.

Another story, but this time probably containing only a kernel of truth, says that Ghazālī took lessons from Khayyām in philosophy in secret. He did so to enable him later, and more authoritatively, to denounce philosophers as heretical. So Khayyām one day installed a drummer on his roof with the instruction that when Ghazālī left the house, he beat his drum vigorously to cause curious neighbours to pour onto the street to discover Ghazālī's deceit. Presumably Khayyām, who was paid by the Shah more generously than some close princes of the blood, lived in an exclusive, governmental district of Isfahān and, there, many people would have recognised Ghazālī, the chancellor's loud theologian. I cannot myself believe that Khayyām would have resorted to such an unbecoming tactic. He did not need to. He was an older man, a highly respected professor of "the sciences of Yūnān", and, as a close friend of the Shah and the Princess Terken, virtually untouchable.[54]

Ghazālī's earliest years are not well attested, but the traditions that have come down to us may explain the flaws in his later behaviour. According to one tradition,[55] he was orphaned soon

---

[54] The tension between the Shah and Grand Vizier Nizām reached such height at one point that the Shah sent an emissary to tell the chancellor: "Do you want me to send soldiers to take your pen and inkpot away? If you think you are my rival, that's another matter". To this, Nizām replied: "Tell the sultan that evidently he hasn't that they would take away his crown if he takes away this pen and inkpot".

[55] This may well be his autobiography which I have not read.

155

after birth in the town of his birth, near today's Mashhad in Khorāsān in north-east Iran, after which his rich clerical relatives placed him and his younger brother Ahmad in the care of a local sūfī. Later, on account of his precocity, he was sent to the cities of Tūs and Nishāpūr for his higher education, with his most important teacher being a famous Ash'arite. Older still, at the age of twenty-three, he was brought to the attention of the Grand Vizier when the latter was in Khorāsān to suppress a rebellion. Nizām al-Mulk, too, was an Ash'arite and favoured fundamentalists for high governmental positions. He took the young man with him to Isfahān and showered him with such flattering titles as "The Light of the Faith".

In return, Ghazālī indulged his new master vigorously. He threw himself into frenetic activity as a campaigning Ash'arite theologian and departmental administrator at a time when the Shah was becoming impatient to exercise power himself and had fallen under the "malign influence of women", as Nizām described the princess's court, that so-called Qarakhānid court that included Khayyām.

Khayyām may well have been instrumental in turning the Shah, several years younger than himself, into a virtual atheist. We have one corroborated story in which the Shah one day grants an audience to Isfahān's chief cleric. The mufti emerges from the court distraught. When his colleagues ask him the reason, he replies: "I am shocked. Our Sultan hasn't heard a word of the Koran. He kept asking me: 'what is this Allah you keep going on about? Tell me his nature!'". It is known that the Shah had refused to learn Arabic, and it is well recorded that later in 1079, he even agreed to let Khayyām announce the reinstatement of all the thirty Zoroastrian day names of each solar month, a practice that even the Sasanians had found impractical and used only for liturgical purposes. (The twelve Zoroastrian month names have, however, survived, even under the present Islamic state.)

156

In 1091, the chancellor appointed Ghazālī to head his most prestigious establishment, the Nizāmiyah college and foundation in Baghdad. This was not to the liking of the caliph al-Moqtadā, but Moqtadā was powerless because he was hated viscerally by the Shah and Terken. They blamed him for the death of their young daughter Māh Malik through mistreatment. Terken had made it a condition of the marriage that Moqtadā sleep with no other woman hence and Moqtadā had violated his vow from the start. Further, and more importantly, the Shah had recently decided that he needed Baghdad from himself as his new winter capital and planned to oust Moqtadā from it. He had already demolished many of the older buildings in the centre of the city and was replacing them with larger, more splendid palaces. He had even designated one of the new palaces for Nizām or whoever might be his next chancellor.

Ghazālī produced some of his most important works over the next two years, despite the fact that his world suddenly appeared to have collapsed. In October the following year, 1092, when the Shah and the chancellor were on their way to Baghdad to spend the winter there, the chancellor was assassinated by a member of the Shiite Ismaili sect, the Nizāris, disguised in the robes of a Sunni cleric. (It happened in my place of birth and upbringing, the small way station of Sahneh in western Iran.) Nizām's powerful sons and his thousands of employees everywhere immediately blamed the Shah for the crime and Malik Shah played into their hands by appointed an implacable enemy of the old man to succeed him. He was the Kurdish Tāj al-Mulk, hitherto the Princess's vizier or chief of staff.

A greater earthquake followed next, one that, in my opinion, paved the way for the First Crusade of 1096-99. Soon after the royal family had settled down in Baghdad, – probably accompanied by their friend and chief physician Khayyām – the Shah fell ill with all the signs of food poisoning and died after a

157

short while on the 19th of November. He was only forty-seven years old and in vigorous health. It was said that he had eaten rotten game during a hunt immediately after his arrival, but the explanation satisfied few people. The danger of rotten meat was well known and the king would have been fed only the freshest food. Thus the death was regarded by the multitude as the revenge of the Nizāmiyah. My own research points in another direction, or perhaps the two in combination. As we have just seen, the caliph had an even stronger reason to dream of the removal of Malik Shah and he had all the resources he needed for the act. His family were infamous for killing many of their own members through poisoning, let alone their other opponents.[56]

Panicked action by Terken then threw the empire into a dynastic war. She hid her husband's corpse for several days to give herself time to seize the treasury and the crown in Isfahān in the name of her four-year-old son, even though Malik Shah had an older son by his other wife. I believe that these events in combination must have brought about the deterioration of Ghazālī's mental health in the following year. As a result of the empire plunging into civil war, the caliph suddenly found himself in a position of power and he disliked Ghazālī and the Ash'aries. All the contenders, too, found themselves in need of more funds and allies, the number one priority being to seek that the blessing of the caliph to claim legitimacy as the new shah. Life at the Nizāmiyah would have suffered drastically, due most probably to the shrinkage of funds and patronage. If I have to guess, I would say that Ghazālī's subsequent spiritual crisis followed almost immediately. At any rate, in July 1095, only eighteen months after the deaths both of Nizām and the Shah, he

---

[56] See Chapter 8 of my biography of Omar Khayyām, pp 187-99.

158

withdrew from his office and left for Damascus, never to return, saying to those around him that he should have never entered the service of princes, that in doing so he had succumbed to his ego. He is said to have concluded that God could not exist, before he found faith once more sometime later. After returning to Nishāpūr via Jerusalem, Mecca and Baghdad, he founded a new khanqah, a sūfi spiritual centre, in that prosperous Khorāsānian city that had remained outside of the war, and devoted his energies to reconciling mysticism and Sunni doctrine. Some years further still, he was persuaded to break his vow. The new sultan, Sanjar, who is reputed to have born a long grudge against Khayyām for giving him up to smallpox in childhood, persuaded him to head the Nizāmiyah college in Nishāpūr. But Ghazālī changed his mind yet again very soon afterwards and returned to his khanqah to write and teach. He wrote an autobiography in which he hid some of the more embarrassing facts of his life, such as his lingering, but secret attachment to Aristotelian metaphysics and Avicennan cosmology. He died in 1111 as a recluse. Khayyām, who also lived in Nishāpūr and was older, survived him by some twenty years, living on to be 83, as opposed to Ghazālī's 53.

Ghazālī, was, at least in his middle, influential years in Isfahān and Baghdad, an extreme determinist. Basing his reasoning on al-Ash'ari's absurd version of atomism, he believed, for example, that when a ball was kicked in a playground, it did not survive into the next moment, for it could not change position due merely to the action of humans. Instead, God created a new ball for each new position as the ball was seen to be moving. He believed that each time we lifted a finger, our action was authorised by God in a new decision by Him, and that He, God, could withdraw His consent any time. This forced Ghazālī, as it had St Augustine long before him, into trying to justify why God punished us for sins that we could not avoid and still remain

159

worthy of our worship. Augustine was, of course, even more unforgiving. He taught that if we were extremely good, God took action to trick us into committing sins so that he could justify punishing us for the sin of our first father, Adam, in sleeping with Eve. If He, God, allowed too many of us into Heaven, there would be no justice in the world. Adam's sin would remain largely unpunished. So, He allowed only a few of us into Heaven due to His own "inscrutable" love. Ghazālī's answer is similar, but perhaps not base quite on the reasoning. He says that whatever decision God takes is just because it is God's decision. God does not have to be just according to our standards. If He were subject to our judgement, the limitation on his freedom would compromise His absolute purity and singularity. Thus whenever God is just according to our judgment, it is because He wants to appear so. Contrast this divine wickedness to Khayyām's expectation of creation if there were to be a creator of the world at all. On balance, he does not seem to have believed in God. In the following quatrains, he trounces an such creator who would allow evil in the world:

Mighty God, when He the world did ordain,
Why did He often from ideal abstain?
Who can be at fault if the tower leans?
If it does not lean, why begin again?

If I had Mazda's omnipotent hand,
I would destroy each and every land.
A whole new world would I then start
In which not a soul nursed a broken heart.[57]

---

[57] My almost verbatim translations. Mazda's is one of the names of God in Zoroastrianism. In the originals, Khayyām uses the other, Yazdān.

160

None of Ghazālī's main opinions, whether or not nonsensical, such as his belief in the existence of nine celestial spheres above us, each with its own intellect and causing the rotation of the sphere below it, are original. But they had widespread and important consequences, both in the world of Islam itself and further afield. In Europe, as I hinted earlier, major figures such as St Aquinas took up his cause against freethinkers faithfully. Aquina's condemnation of Averroes is in large part a repeat of Ghazālī's Tahāfut al-Falāsifah, the Incoherence of the Philosophers. For this reason, I believe that The Tahāfut is the most important of all of Ghazālī's extant works.

In it, Ghazālī does not condemn philosophy as such, only the philosophers who are not Muslims or have, in his opinion, deviated from a literal interpretation of the Koran and the hadīth. Indeed, he stresses our need to learn philosophy's methods to think clearly, to be able to interpret the Koran and the hadīth correctly, and to be able better to point out the mistaken ways of the philosophers in accordance with the standards of proof that they set for themselves. The philosophers he has in mind are principally Avicenna and Fārābī. These he dislikes particularly because, while they called themselves Muslims, he regards them as having given up core Islamic beliefs and rituals. He disagrees with two of Avicenna's teachings especially: 1) that God knows only universals, not individuals, and 2), that after death, human bodies, when resurrected, could not possibly host their souls[58]. He also lines up three central beliefs to distinguish a Muslim from an unbeliever. These are monotheism, the prophethood of Muhammad, and life after death as depicted vividly in the Koran. Apostates from Islam must be punished with death.

---

[58] See the entry on Ghazālī in the Stanford Encyclopedia of Philosophy by Frank Griffel, 2020.

The Tahāfut is in the form of twenty areas of contention in which Ghazālī confronts the philosophers' errors, as he sees them. He accuses them of unreason, for he says that none of their twenty claims that he examines can be proven through demonstration, as they claim. The right way is to consult scripture and to interpret it rationally, rationally, of course, according to his own notions of rationality. He says, rightly in many cases, that they rely on the authority of their predecessors, but then resorts to authority himself, the authority of prophets. He says that the earliest philosophers had acquired metaphysical truths because the earliest prophets had revealed those truths to them. But later they claimed that they had come by those truths through reason, which was impossible.

Some modern commentators claim that, unwittingly, Ghazālī helped in further naturalising philosophy in the Islamic world, that in truth he was a staunch Aristotelian who approved of the Greek sage's attachment to empiricist rationalism. One such thinker is Professor Frank Griffel of Yale and Oxford. In a recent work he states:

> Al-Ghazālī is indeed the first Muslim theologian who actively promotes the naturalisation of the philosophical tradition into Islamic theology. His works document an attempt to integrate Aristotelian logics into the tradition of *Kalām,* of rationalist Islamic theology.

In other words, if I am not mistaken, Ghazālī borrowed Aristotelian logic with which better to combat the philosophers. It is an old instinct. Steal you enemy's sword with which to kill him, except that in this case, it does not appear too logical to rely on the proclamations of shamans and prophets to prove your point. Professor Griffel adds: "some critics and interpreters of al-Ghazālī have questioned how he could make use of Aristotelian logics without also adopting Aristotelian ontology … a specific explanation of the world's most elementary

162

constituents and their relations to one another. The answer is that Ghazālī understood the connection very well. However, he was less open about this. In his autobiography, he turns his criticism of metaphysics to the fore and mentions his appreciation of [the philosophers'] teachings only in the passing."[59]

I think that we would be on safer ground to say that the force of Ghazālī's loud condemnation of the philosophers came across to his audiences more clearly than did his nuances regarding the attractions of philosophy confessed during his less combative moments. This has largely been the verdict of earlier commentators on him. There remain voices to the contrary, but there is no unanimity. My own view is in step with the previous generations of observers, that Ghazālī has for a long time been the favourite theologian of fundamentalist Sunni activists precisely because he was true to their literalist cause. In his fight against the individual exercising his own intellect, he proved effective because he was eloquent and charismatic and resorted to outwardly attractive profundities. He sounded knowledgeable. He was the prophetic voice that the masses needed.

I have already mentioned that Ghazālī advocated capital punishment for those Muslims who gave up their inherited religion. Elsewhere, too, he issues some extreme opinions. Though he was brought up in the province of Khorāsān, a province that had recently fallen under the spell of Ferdowsi's Shāhnāmeh – the epic of the kings and emperors of pre-Islamic Iran – he advocated that every effort be made to marginalise the speaking of Persian because it was not the language of the Koran and helped to divert the attention of Muslims elsewhere. He urged rulers that all popular Iranian festivities, such as the

---

[59] Al-Ghazālī's Philosophical Theology, Oxford University Press, 2009. P10.

Norouz spring festival, be banned. They kept alive the memory of the Zoroastrians. It is said that he was of Iranian extraction. I am not convinced. Large numbers of Arabs had settled in Khorāsān since the seventh century conquest. But even if the claim is true, it appears as if he had been brought up by his clerical relatives to believe that the Arabs were a superior race simply because they were the people of the prophet. He was, in effect, an Arab nationalist in the guise of Muslim universalism. Nor would he have been a rare specimen of the kind. Many Iranian, Syrian and Egyptian clerics have since the advent of Islam invented Arab descent for themselves.[60]

But should we agree with some who have said that Ghazālī "closed the door of ijtihad for ever? (Ijtihād means, literally, to make a "personal effort" to arrive at the right decision when Koranic guidelines are not clear)

I am not certain, and he would not have not used the phrase, for ijtihad is said to have been approved by Muhammed. What we can be certain about is that he used the power of his mentor Grand Vizier Nizām – and the rage of the city mob – to silence any contemporaries who disagreed with a literalist reading of the Koran and the Sunna (the hadith traditions of the deeds and sayings of Muhammad). The obvious historical example here is Khayyām. Khayyam was forced to give up teaching philosophy at the height of Ghazālī's activism in Isfahān, despite many students begging of him not to do so, and when he went into self-

---

[60] In return, other Iranians have invented a pejorative phrase to describe them. It is: "Seyyede khar jasteh", meaning a stranger who jumps down from his donkey as he arrives in a village where he is unknown and tells the locals that he is a direct descendant of the holy prophet, a "seyyed". He is believed and suddenly becomes a revered figure. Among Shiites, they are distinguishable by their black turbans.

imposed exile in the city of Shiraz in 1081, I am confident as his biographer that it was an expediency most probably urged on him by Malik Shah. Being away from the court in Isfahān for a few months might allay the fears of the clergy that the king had become an unbeliever under malign influences.

When asking ourselves whether Ghazālī was the most important agent in causing the "closing of the door of ijtihad" in Islam in the years that straddled the eleventh and twelfth centuries, it might be wise to examine other possible factors, also. One such factor ought to be the vast First Crusade of 1096-99 that culminated in the conquest of Jerusalem by a west-European army and the establishment of Latin principalities in Syria for the first time since the Islamic conquests of the seventh century. The success of the invasions shocked the Muslim world and caused a diversion of funds into the military, away from the institutions of learning. Then arrived the Mongols who inflicted unprecedented destruction on eastern Islam and put a final end to what remained of the pretence of an Abbāsid caliphate in Baghdad. This was followed in its turn by the re-awakening of the spirit of the ancient Greeks and Romans in what later became known as the Renaissance movement in north-western Europe whose military, artistic, industrial and scientific brilliance further deepened the Muslims' growing despair and weakened their lack of confidence in their civilisation. Combined together, these catastrophes had a numbing, even a paralysing, effect on them and persuaded their intellectual leaders that the solution lay in withdrawing into themselves, seek inspiration in the triumphs of the deeds of the prophet and the rightful caliphs, erect taller barriers against the outside world. Ghazālī's voice was a high-sounding interpretation of the core doctrines of Islam that gave Muslim fundamentalists justification in the positions they had adopted. But it may be rash to claim that, without him, the course of subsequent intellectual history among Muslims, particularly

165

the Sunnis, would have been significantly different. This is despite the fact that, unlike sane Averroes, he continued to be followed widely by opinion-makers among Muslims long after his death.

Postscript

At the end of this investigation, I would like my readers to ask themselves whether or not the following statement is correct: "The primary curse that afflicted the philosophical thought of all pre-modern peoples was their scientific ignorance resulting in their inability to see that the universe did not revolve around the Earth, and therefore around us". It followed naturally for them to think that the chief reason for the world existing at all was the well-being of us humans. We were clearly superior to other animals and must be meant to be their masters, for we were unique in our power of reasoning and thus our ability to build civilisations. In their cosy world, bereft of the scientific method and the powerful instruments of measurement that science has produced recently, they were even more innocent of the inner workings of the universe – let alone its unimaginable extent – as are today's primary school children. Thus did struggle in abject darkness such brilliant minds as Aristotle and Avicenna, Aquinas and Scotus.

All this left our ancestors at the mercy of what they could see with their naked eyes and deduce from observing the behaviour of their peers and animals. They were vulnerable to shamans and prophets who told them tall tales of how the world had come into being and for what purposes. Fārābī told his adoring audiences that the soul lived in the brain. In the following century, Avicenna taught his students that it lived in the heart and the principle arteries around it. Could they not see that the heart of a dead sheep, when thrown onto hot ashes, began to beat again? Was that not a sign that it was conscious?

It helped the shaman if he were endowed with charisma and exuded self-confidence, and it helped him if, in propounding his unequalled knowledge beliefs, he used profound words that few

167

among in his audience understood. He could also exploit with profit the sage words of the revered patriarchs of the past.

And yet, and yet, here I am, myself, having just spent sixteen months of my precious last years researching the sage words of those same revered patriarchs of the past. Has it not been a complete waste of time? Should anyone care to read it? I cannot help, but wonder. Is it useful for us to know, for example, that Māni claimed he had ascended to heaven, or that Fārābī believed iron could be transmuted into gold?

We may here compare and contrast philosophers and scientists. It is well known and often proclaimed that a scientist does not need to know the history of his specialism to function at the very forefront of it. Chemists, for example, to whose ranks I once belonged, do not need to know what agonies their predecessors suffered in their efforts to explain why physical reality behaved the way it did. In fact, they would be held back if they spent even an hour on such retrospection. By contrast, philosophers, do not deal with mysteries that can be measured and tested. They deal with issues that are abstract and may have several answers or none at all from the stand point of the person who investigates them. If they are not to repeat themselves, they need many years of retrospection in the history of their subject, as well as an adequate knowledge of the latest science of their time, with any question that they solve to general agreement immediately branching off from philosophy – as we define it today – to become a new science. For example, whether the world is eternal or not is now for nuclear physicists on which to pronounce. But there is one more difference between a history of philosophy and a history of chemistry. Telling the history of philosophy is another form of telling the history of humanity.

I was once asked by an interviewer - probably on BBC Radio 4 – which single book I would take to a prison island with me if I were allowed only one volume. My ready answer was: Bertrand Russell's History of Western Philosophy. That tome of a book has never stopped being out of print since its first publication in the wake of the Second World War, and in a hundred languages. Nor is it being bought by philosophers only. It is not a handbook of research. It generalises in too many places and has many blemishes that would mislead a researcher. Yet we can, with confidence, describe it as one of the most-loved documents ever written. Telling the story of the evolution of our ancestors' thinking, as it does, it reminds us of a famous saying by Aristotle: "Humans, by nature, want to know", and if it is about our forebears, all the more curious we become. There is much evidence to prove this point if we look around us. Book shelves in all serious bookshops and libraries bend under the weight of books devoted to the history of ideas. We seem to have an innate need to know how the generations that went before us, strived to arrive at a better view.

Appendix: Avicenna's autobiography

(Completed by his student Abu Obaid Gūzgānī)

What follows in this appendix needs an explanation and a warning. Its first and smaller part, by Avicenna himself, suggests that it was written in haste, or even dictated to a secretary. If so, it is most likely that its original form was in Persian, not Arabic, and written, or dictated, as was Avicenna's habit, after midnight and after heavy drinking. It even has the feeling of an after-dinner conversation. We know that the great man, who was by then the grand vizier of a sizable state based on Isfahān, was extremely busy and – by the confession of Abu Obaid Gūzgānī, his long-time student and assistant at whose request he provided it, a heavy drinker. Thus it may not be accurate everywhere, for example in the dating and sequence of his books.

The second part, by Gūzgānī, however, which completes the life, seems more reliable, because he says he wrote it after Avicenna's death, presumably at leisure. If one or both parts were in Persian, we can be confident that Gūzgānī later translated them into Arabic for a wider sale himself, for it would have been in demand. It was the story of a most famous man.

Whatever the minutiae, though, the document sheds light on Avicenna's works, as well as on his life as physician, statesman and philosopher.

Three Arabic manuscripts of the document have survived, but not as stand-alone documents. They are included within the books of three Arab historians later. I do not have access to these and so have translated a version in Persian which was made by an Iranian scholar at Tehran University, the late Professor Sayyed Sadegh Gowharīn. As such, therefore, the combination of autobiography and biography has passed through several

171

lenses and probably also suffered from most of the hazards that haunt the copying of old manuscripts for preservation or sale.

Having made these reservations, both Avicenna and Gūzgānī appear to have tried hard to be factual, rather than propagandistic. Avicenna's account is a little precocious, as one might expect of a former mathematical prodigy who had risen to be a powerful minister of state. But his memory had not deteriorated due to age or alcohol. He died in his early – or middle – 50s and seemed still at the height of his intellectual powers. As for Gūzgānī, is account appears to be based on a combination of diary notes and research. Nor is he uncritical of his late master, despite his touching loyalty to him as employer, teacher and friend. For example, he criticises Avicenna for his voracious indulgence in frequent sex (presumably with women who seem mostly to have been either prostitutes or slaves. This aspect of Avicenna's personality, too, is revealing, as well as revolting. There are no suggestions that he ever encumbered himself with the responsibilities of a husband or father).

I have translated the two texts in full for those readers who may have a professional interest in them. In places, the accounts also paint a vivid picture of the political upheavals that afflicted Greater Khorāsān [Central Asia], Iran and Iraq. Here they are:

My father was of [the city] of Balkh. During the reign of [the Sāmāian king] Nūh ibn Mansūr, he emigrated to Bukhārā and entered that sovereign's service. They gave him the management of the town of Kharmethan, which was one of the bigger towns of the region. Nearby was another town,

172

Afshana. My father married a woman from that town and my brother and I were born to her[61].

Then we all returned to Bukhārā and my father employed for me a teacher for the Koran and literature. By the age of ten I had learnt the Koran and much of the literature. From the start, there were signs in me that amazed my teachers.

By the invitation of an Ismā'ili missionary, my father joined that religion and I learned from them some points about the soul and intellect, as they believed them to be. My brother had also joined the religion and often I listened to their discussions. I understood them, but my heart wasn't wholly in what they said, even though they described me as of them. Sometimes, too, they discussed philosophy, geometry, Indian arithmetic, and the like, until my father sent me to a green grocer who knew Indian arithmetic well, for further instruction.

At this time, Abu Abdallah Nātelī came to Bukhārā and my father brought him to live in our house in the hope of his teaching me philosophy. Before him, I had been attending jurisprudence classes under Ismā'il Zāhed, a famous teacher of that science, [and I continued doing so] until I became an expert in such discussions and reasonings and techniques of debate as were current among that people [the Ismā'ilis].

Then I studied the Isagoge [Porphyry's introduction to Aristotle's categories of entities] and when he told me of the definition ["hadd"] of genera, which is a discussion on various types, I did some research on it on my own. Nātelī had never heard of such detail and was very surprised. He began to advise my father that no profession be chosen for me other than science. Whatever subject Nātelī chose, I

---

[61] Her name is reported elsewhere to have been Setāreh, meaning star.

understood it better than he did. Eventually I gathered an adequate knowledge of logic, for he did not know enough of it.

After that I studied books on my own and read on many topics until I learnt the details of logic thoroughly. I also studied five or six of the puzzles in Euclid under Nātelī and solved the rest on my own. Then, still under Nātelī, I began the Almagest [Ptolemy's register of the motions of the stars and planets], but as I finished the preliminaries and reached the geometrical drawings, Nātelī said: "Now study it on your own and solve its problems. I will correct you if you've made a mistake". There were so many problems he hadn't encountered before and I had to teach him their solutions; at which time he left for Gorgānj and I began to study books on the natural sciences and on theology. So, every day more doors of knowledge open up to me.

Subsequently I turned to medicine and read numerous books and articles on it and learned that it was not a difficult science. I mastered it in a short time, so much so that famous scientists and philosophers and physicians began to study it under me. Also I began to treat patients and accumulated much experience. At the same time I did not neglect jurisprudence. By this time I was sixteen years old.

I spent another year-and-a-half on logic and all other aspects of philosophy. All the time, day and night I did not rest. From dusk to dawn I studied and all day I was restless unless I was studying. Whenever I couldn't solve a problem, I went to the mosque and prayed to the First Source for help. In the evening I would return home and light the lamp and continue to read and write until sleep overcame me or exhaustion defeated me. Then I would drink a little wine to regain my strength. Often as I fell asleep, the problems would return to me and many of their solutions I found in my dreams.

174

I continued in this way till I gained confidence in all the sciences and learnt all that was possible for man to learn. Whatever I learnt in those years, I still remember precisely. And so it was that in logic, the naturals and mathematics I learnt whatever there was to learn, so much so that, until today, I haven't been able to add to it.

Then I returned to theology and began [Aristotle's] Metaphysics, but did not understand much of it. I read it again and again and still failed. I read it more than forty times, until I could recite it by heart, but still didn't understand it. I lost heart and told myself that there was no way into that book, until, one evening in the bazaar of the booksellers, I was offered a book. I turned it down, thinking it worthless. But the seller insisted. He said it was extremely cheap because the owner needed the money. He offered it to me for three dirhams only. I bought it. It was by Fārābī and called On the Metaphysics.

I returned home and began to read it. I already knew the words. Suddenly their meanings became clear. I was very pleased. The next day I gave a fortune in alms to the poor.

The king, Nūh ibn Mansūr, was now afflicted with a disease that his physicians could not cure and so they had mentioned my name to him, as by then I was known among the doctors for prolific reading. So he called me in and I took part in treating him with his other doctors until [in 997AD] he recovered. One day I asked him for permission to visit the royal library, for its medical books. He agreed and they took me there. I found a large library with many rooms, with each room full of shelves on which books were paced nearly and systematically. One room was confined to the Arabic language, another to poetry, yet another to jurisprudence, etc. In some rooms were held books on specific sciences, and the whole library had an index. I inspected the index and chose what I needed. There were many books of which I had

175

never heard, nor seen similar ones elsewhere, nor did I see books like them afterwards. I discovered their strengths and learned the worth of every man in the sciences and philosophy.

By now I was eighteen years old and had memorised all the books that interested me. I haven't added to my knowledge since. The only difference is that at that time I learned more quickly, while today the sciences that I have learnt are combined in my mind together so that I have a more clear vision of them. Otherwise, fact is fact.

In my neighbourhood, there lived a man called Abul-Hasan Arūdī. He asked me to write an all-inclusive book for him. I did so and made a gift of it to him. I called it Al-Majmū', The Compendium. All the sciences were described in it, except mathematics. By then I was twenty-one years old. Another neighbour was a man called Abu Bakr Baraqī. He was famously pious and regarded as unrivalled in jurisprudence and [Koranic] commentary. He asked me to write a book on philosophy for him. It came to twenty volumes and I called it The Available and the Valid [Al-Hāsel wal-Mahsūl]. Also for him I wrote a book on ethics. I called it Piety and Sin [Al-Birr wal-Ithm]. Those two books are only with him now. I didn't give them to anyone to copy. Then my father died and my life fell apart. I had to enter government service. Not long afterwards, by necessity, I had to leave Bukhārā. [62] I left for Gorgānj, where a lover of science and philosophy by the name of Abul-Hasan Sohaili

---

[62] This was probably just before or shortly after 999, when the Persian Sāmānids in Bukhārā fell to the Karakhānid Turks from central Asia. The latter were fanatical Sunnis to begin with and thus intolerant of the Ismā'ili Shiites to whose ranks Avicenna belonged, at least officially.

was the vizier. By his commendation I found a position at the court of Ali ibn Ma'mūn. I was in the ranks of the clergy then, with the long robe and tailed turban. They gave me a salary worthy of the position.

Then, [again] by necessity, I had to leave. I went to Nasā, then to Bāvard, followed by Tūs, Bashghān, Samangān and Jājrom on the borders of Khorāsān, eventually arriving in Gorgān. All the way my aim was to reach the court of the Amīr Qābūs. But when I arrived, I found that his soldiers had overthrown him and imprisoned him in one of his own castles. He died there. When I was passing through Dehestān [near Nishāpūr], I fell severely ill and had to return to Gorgān. It was there that Abu Obaid Gūzgānī joined me. I wrote a poem describing my situation at the time. It includes this line: There is no city big enough for me: / My price is high; I find no buyers!

Here ends Avicenna's text and begins Gūzgānī'ssupplement, written at an unknown date after his master's death[63]):

In Gorgān there was a man by the name of Abu Muhammad Shīrāzī who loved this type of science. He bought a house in his own neighbourhood for the Sheikh and stationed him there, and it was there that I began to study the Almagest under the Sheikh. It was also there that he wrote the book Al-Mokhtasar al-Awāsit (The Summary of the Middles) for me.[64] Also he wrote the two books Al-Mabda' wal-Mo'ād

---

[63] Gūzgānī, or Juzjāni in Arabic, survived Avicenna three more decades, dying in 1070 and asking to be buried beside his master in Hamadān.

[64] Aristotle's Golden Mean priciple.

(The Beginning and the End[65]) and Al-Ersād al-Kolliyah (A General [astronomical] Survey) for Shīrāzī. Also there the Master began many of his other books, such as the Qānūn (Canon of Medicine) and the Mokhtasar al-Magest (A Summary of the Almagest). Others he began during his subsequent journey to Ray.

In Ray, he was received by the Lady and her son [King] Majd ad-Dowla. Both honoured him generously due to all the correspondence that had been exchanged between them previously. The King contracted melancholia and an attack of the bile. The Master began his treatment until he recovered. At the same time he wrote the book Al-Muād (Life after Death).

Later on, after the defeat and death of Helāl ibn Badr Hasanuyah[66] and the invasion of the armies of Baghdad, the Sheikh decided to leave Ray and go over to Shams ed-Dawlah [the prince's brother in Hamadān]. He found that first he had to go to Qazvīn before he could journey to Hamadān. There he was received by the Kad Bānū ("Senior Lady"). She made certain that the Sheikh would be provided with all comforts. The king heard of his presence and called for him. He suffered from abdominal pain. The Sheikh cured him and the king rewarded him with expensive robes. The Sheikh spent around forty days and nights by the king's bed, after which the king returned him to his home with great gratitude and made him one of his companions. A little later, the king went to war against Anāz and took the Sheikh with him, but the war resulted in defeat and they returned to Hamadān.

---

[65] Mu'ād is also means the promised life after death.

[66] The Hasanuyah were a Kurdish dynasty who ruled large territories straddling present western Iran and eastern Iraq.

Shams ed-Dawlah asked the Sheikh to become his vizier and the Sheikh accepted. However, subsequently, the army rebelled over unpaid wages and promotions and blamed it on the Sheikh. They ransacked his house and seized all they found there. They also imprisoned him and demanded that the King execute him. But the king refused. He only dismissed him from the ministry. The Sheikh now went into hiding in the home of Abu Sa'īd bin Dokhdūk, until the king's abdominal pains returned and he was again called to the court. The king apologised for the dismissal and once again appointed him his vizier.

It was then that I asked him to write for me an introduction to the books of Archimedes. He said: I have no time for that, but, if you wish, I can write an outline of the intellectual [non-mathematical?] sciences for you, without going into the details of why I refute their opponents. I agreed.

He began with the naturals and called it the Shifā' (The Healing). He also wrote the first book of the Canon [of Medicine].

As he did not have enough time by day, in the evenings we his students and others eager on the sciences would gather at his home. I would recite from the Healing and others from the Canon. Afterwards, after [most of] the students had left, musicians and singers would arrive and we would eat and drink wine.

His teaching in the evenings was a rest and distraction from the preoccupations of the day in the service of the Amīr. In this manner some time passed until the Amīr went to war [against a rebellion] in Tārem [west of Isfahān]. But there his pains returned and, as he had ignored the Sheikh's orders, he was afflicted by other illnesses, too. His troops decided to return him home, but he died on the way, upon which his son and successor [Samā ed-Dowla] asked the Sheikh to continue in the vizierate. But the Sheikh refused. Instead, in

179

secret, he wrote to Alā ed-Dowla [in Isfahān] asking to enter his service. By this time he was in hiding in the home of Abu Qālib the Perfumer and I urged him to use his time to finish the Healing. He summoned Abu Qālib and asked for ink and paper. He made notes on the chief topics over eight days. He then spent another two days expanding on the notes, until it was all completed, without his having access to any books. It was all done from memory. Then he put the notes before him and began the details and the explanations. Every day he would write around fifty pages, until he completed all the sciences, except De Anima and the Plants.

Subsequently he turned to the Logic and made some progress there until Tāj al-Molk [the new vizier] accused him of being in correspondence with Alā ed-Dowla and ordered his agents to find him. This they did when some of the Sheikh's enemies betrayed him. He was arrested and imprisoned in a castle. There he wrote a poem that contains this line: In my being here, there is no doubt. / The question is: How do I get out!

[Fortunately], Alā ed-Dowla invaded [from Isfahān] and the vizier Tāj al-Molk was thrown in prison in that same castle. However, Alā ed-Dowla left for Isfahān and Tāj al-Molk and Samā ed-Dowla returned to repossess Hamadān. They brought the Sheikh with them. He lived in the home of Alavi and resumed the writing of the Logic part of the Healing. When he was still in prison, he had written the books Al-Hedāyāt [The Gifts] and Qolanj [ulcerative colitis?], and the monograph Hayy bin Yaqdhān [Alive, son of Awake]. He had written the book Al-Adwiyat al-Qalbiyah [Herbs for for the Heart?] previously, on his first arrival in Hamadān.

The vizier continued to encourage the Sheikh [to remain in Hamadān] with generous promises. But he decided to move to Isfahān. As a result, he and I and his brother [Mahmoud]

180

and two slaves[67] disguised ourselves as Sūfis and slipped out un-noticed. We suffered many hardships on the way until, eventually, we arrived as Tayrān, one of the gates of Isfahān. There we found some of the Sheikh's friends, as well as some of the king's men, waiting for us. The king had sent the Sheikh an expensive suit and a fine mount. In the city, they had prepared the house of Abdollah bin Bābī for him, with fine rugs and furnishings.

The Sheikh then attended the king and received an extraordinarily grand welcome. The king decided that there be a weekly gathering of top scientists, philosophers and jurists at court every Friday, so that they could debate issues. The Sheikh attend them.

In Isfahān the Sheikh decided on finishing the Shifā' and completed the Logic and the Almagest. He summarised Euclid, Arithmetic and Music and in each mathematical book he inserted additions where he thought it useful. At the end of the Almagest he added astronomical information no-one knew previously, and he inserted some criticisms of Euclid. So the Shifā' was finished in this way, except De Anima and the Plants which he finished in the year when the king decided to go to Shāpūr. On the way there, he finished the book the Najāt [the Salvation].

The Sheikh was constantly in attendance to Alā ed-Dowla and was considered among his closest friends. When the King decided to go to Hamadān, the Sheikh went with him. One night the conversation drifted onto astronomy and the Sheikh mentioned the inaccuracies that had crept into the calendars due to the age of the registers. Alā ed-Dowla asked him to turn his attention to the matter. All the costs would be

---

[67] The word used is "qolām". They might have been contracted servants.

181

provided. So the Sheikh asked for me and told me immediately to start setting up a new observatory and employ experts and buy equipment. But then many problems and distractions arose and the work was stopped. The Sheikh himself wrote the Alā'ī Encyclopaedia [the Dāneshnāmeh Alā'ī in Persian and dedicated to him].

One day, there was a discussion on literature in the presence of the king and the Sheikh expressed his opinion on something when Abu Mansūr Jebā'ī turned on him and said: "You are a philosopher and scientist and don't know much about the art of language and its branches. It's not becoming of you to intervene on such matters." This caused the Sheikh to turn to the study of books on language and literature and this continued for three years. He asked that the book by Abī Mansūr Azharī be brought to him from Khorāsān and eventually surpassed all other experts. He wrote three poems and three books in the style of three famous writers: ibn Amīd, Sābī and Sāhib. He ordered that the three books be disguised in old bindings and plotted secretly with the king that he, the king, show them to Abu Mansūr for his opinion. On the chosen day, the king showed the books to Abu Mansūr and told him he had come across them during a hung in the country. Who might be their authors? Abu Mansūr took the books and spent some time studying them. Many aspects of them defeated him. When he reported back to the king and [admitting his failures], the Sheikh entered as arranged with the king and resolved the problems. All those present were astonished and Abu Mansūr, who was famous for pride and self-aggrandisement, realised that the documents were the sheikh's own work and had been written in retaliation for his brashness [three years ago]. He was ashamed and apologised to the Sheikh. Subsequently the Sheikh wrote the book Lisān el-Arab [The Arabic Tongue], the like of which no-one had seen to that day. But it has not been transcribed into clean copies and nor has anyone risen to the task [of copying it?] since the Sheikh's death.

The Sheikh was an extremely experienced physician and was planning to expand the Canon. Unfortunately all his notes for it perished. One of those experiences was that once day the Sheikh was having a severe headache and felt that a liquid was about to penetrate the membrane in his head. So he asked for ice and cloth and wrapped the ice around his head until the membrane strengthened and prevented the liquid from bursting through. Another was of a woman in Khwārazm who had contracted consumption. The Sheikh prescribed that she eat nothing except golqand [rose petal marmalade]. She ate a hundred mans of it [about 300 kilograms or six barrels?] and was cured.[68]

The sheikh wrote Mokhtasar al-Asqar [The Shorter Summary] on logic in Gorgān. This is the same book that appears at the beginning of The Salvation. A copy reached Shiraz and a group of the philosophers there, including the chief judge, raised some objections to it. They put this into a booklet and sent it, with a letter, to Abul-Qāsem Sāheb Ebrāhīm ben Bābā Dailamī[69], in Isfahan, so that he would show it to the Sheikh. One day in the evening, a very hot evening, Sheikh Abul-Qāsem arrived at the Sheikh's residence and gave him the letter and the booklet. The Sheikh read the letter and gave it back. He then put the booklet in front of him and while others present went on

---

[68] Poor woman! The placebo effect may have consoled her for a time, but she had obviously not contracted tuberculosis and depriving her of a varied diet weakened her defences against other diseases, not to mention trebling her weight.

[69] Here I use the spelling of Arabic words as Persians pronounce them, for example Sāheb instead of Sāhib.

conversing, he stared at the contents. When Abul-Qāsem had left, he told me to prepare papers for him for five booklets, each of ten pages in Pharaonic [large] format. After the Eshā' [mid-evening] prayer, he pulled the candles forward and asked for wine. He asked me and his brother to sit down with him and he began to write and continued to drink till about midnight, when his brother and I were overcome by sleep. He allowed us to leave. But at dawn, someone was knocking on my door. It was the Sheikh's servant. He wanted me. I hurried to his presence. He was still sitting up. He gave me the booklets he had written and told me to take them to Abul-Qāsem without delay. He added: "Tell him I've hurried writing them so that they can be sent with this morning's caravan". When I took them to Abul-Qāsem, he was astonished, and so was the man who had brought the message from Shiraz. The story spread to the bazaar and became history.

The Sheikh invented some instruments for the observatory I mentioned above, and wrote a number of treatises [on astronomy] for it. I spent some eight years afterwards on the matter. I wanted to master Ptolemy. Eventually I did this, more or less.

The Sheikh wrote the book Al-Insāf [Fair Judgement]. When the forces of Sultan Mas'ūd invaded Isfahān, they ransacked the Sheikh's house and the book was lost.

The Shiekh was a strong man. He never tired. He womanised in the extreme. He had complete confidence in the strength of his health. But the frequent indulgence in sex gradually weakened him, so that in the year when the Amīr went to war against Amīr Tāsh Farrāsh and took the Sheikh with him, the Sheikh contracted a severe qolanj [ulcerative colitis?]. One day, for fear of the war resulting in Alā ed-Dowla's defeat and his own not being able to flee due to the illness, he ordered that he be treated with the hoqnah [an injection of a herbal lotion into the rectum] eight times. As a result, he became severely diarrhetic and, as he had to accompany the king to Izajj [a town in the south], epileptic attacks compounded the qolanj. He continued the injections. One day he ordered that they use two portions of celery seeds, in order to reduce the emanations. One of the physicians had used five portions, instead. I was not there and therefore I cannot say if it were deliberate. But this made the diarrhoea even more severe. The Sheikh was at this time also taking metroditus. But one of his servants who had stolen from him had added a great deal of opium to the metroditus. In this condition they took him back to Isfahān. He was so weak by then that he could not rise or stand. There he continued to treat himself and improved enough to attend the king. But still he did not rein in his urges. He did not reduce his womanising, until the king went to war against Hamadān and the Sheikh accompanied him. On the way, the illness returned. In Hamadān he realised the disease had gone too far. He stopped taking remedies. He said: "The manager cannot manage any more". A few days later he died. He lived fifty-three years. The date of his birth was 375 of the Hijra and the date of his death 428.

Bibliography

Adamson, Peter: *Philosophy in the Islamic World.* Oxford: OUP, 2016.

Adamson, Peter, and Di Giovanni, Matteo (ed.): *Interpreting Averroes: Critical Essays.* Cambridge: CUP, 2019.

Anthony, David W: *The Horse, the Wheel and Language.* Princeton: Princeton University Press, 2007.

Arberry, Prof. A. J. (ed.): *The Legacy of Persia.* Oxford: OUP, 1953.

Arnaldez, Roger, translated by David Streight: *Averroes: A Rationalist in Islam.* University of Notre Dame Press, Indiana, 2000.

Avicenna (Ibn Sina): *The Metaphysics of the Healing.* Provo, Utah: Brigham Young University Press. 2005.

Charles River Editors: *The Religion of Mesopotamia.* Harvard University, online.

Cottingham, John (ed). *Western Philosophy: An Anthology.* Third Edition. Oxford: Blackwell Publishing. 2021.

Baumer, Christoph: *The History of Central Asia: The Age of Islam and the Mongols.* Bloomsbury, 2016.

Boardman, Sir John. *Persia and the West: An Archaeological Investigation of the Genesis of Achaemenid Art.* London: Thames & Hudson, 2000.

Boyce, Mary. *Zoroastrians: Their Religious Beliefs and Practices.* London: Routledge, 2001, 2nd Edition.

Daryaee, Touraj. *Sasanian Persia: The Rise and Fall of an Empire.* London: I. B. Tauris, 2009.

Duchesne-Guillemin, Jacques. *The Hymns of Zarathustra.* London: John Murray, 1952.

Fernandez-Morera, Dario: *The Myth of the Andalusian Paradise.* Wilmington, Delaware: Intercollegiate Studies Institute, 2016.

Ferdowsi. Shahnameh. Early eleventh century).

Ghirshman, Roman.: *Iran: From the Earliest Times to the Islamic Conquest.* Harmondsworth, Middlesex: Penguin books, 1954.

Gowharin, Sayyed Sadegh: *Abu Ali Sina.* Tehran. 1968.

Griffel, Frank, *Al-Ghazālī's Philosophical Theology.* Oxford: OUP, 2009.

Haldon, John. *Byzantium: A History.* Stroud, Gloucestershire: Tempus, 2000.

187

Herodotus. *The Histories.*

Howard-Johnson, James. *Witnesses to a World Crisis: Historians and Histories of the Middle East in the Seventh Century.* Oxford: OUP, 2010.

Katouzian, Homa. *The Persians.* New Haven and London: Yale University Press, 2009.

Kennedy, Hugh. *The Court of the Caliphs.* London: Weidenfeld and Nicholson, 2004.

Kenny, Anthony. *A New History of Western Philosophy.* Oxford: OUP.

Kosmin, Paul J. *Time and its Adversaries in the Seleucid Empire.* Harvard University Press, 2018.

Kramer, Samuel Noah. *The Sumerians: Their history, culture and character.* The University of Chicago Press, Chicago and London, 1963.

Kriwaczek, Paul: *In Search of Zarathustra.* London: Phoenix, 2002.

Lewis, Bernard. *The Arabs in History.* Oxford: OUP, 1992.

Mallory, J. P. *In Search of the Indo-Europeans.* New York: Thames & Hudson, 1989.

Marozzi, Justin. *Islamic Empires.* London: Allen Lane, 2019.

----- *Captives and Companions: A History of Slavery and the Slave Trade in the Islamic World.* London: Allen Lane, forthcoming, July 2025.

Nasr, Seyyed Hossein, and Leaman, Oliver. *History of Islamic Philosophy.* London and New York: Routledge, 1996.

Nizām al-Mulk. *Siasatnameh (Politics – 1080s).* Tehran: Zavvar.

O'Hear, Anthony. *The Prism of Truth: Reflections on Myth.* Cascade Books, Eugene, Oregon. 2024.

Ormsby, Eric. *Ghazali: The Revival of Islam.* Oxford: One World. 2008.

Penrose, Roger: *Fashion, Faith and Fantasy in the New Physics of the Universe.* Princeton and Oxford: Princeton University Press. 2016.

Pirnia, Hasan & Iqbal, Abbas. *Tarikh e Iran.* Tehran: Khayyam Publications, 1987.

Plato. *Nomoi, Timaeus, The Republic.*

Plutarch. *The Lives of Notable Grecians and Romans.*

Pourshariati, Parvaneh. *Decline and Fall of the Sasanian Empire.* London: I. B. Tauris, 2020.

Razī, Hāshem. *Avestā: Kohantarin Ganjīneye Maktūbe Irāne Bāstān*. Tehran: Behjat Publications, 2009.

Rezazadeh-Malek, Rahim. *Daneshnameh Khayyami (The complete works of Omar Khayyam)*. Tehran. 1998.

Renfrew, Colin. *Archaeology & Lnaguage: The Puzzle of Indo-European Origins*. London: Jonathan Cape, 1987.

Rovelli, Carlo. *Anaximander and the Nature of Science*. London: Allan Lane. 2023.

Russell, Bertrand. *History of Western Philosophy*. London: Unwin University Books, 1969.

Sasanfar, Abtine. *Avestā: Bagardāne Haft Hāt az Avestā*. Paris: Editions Khavaran, 2003.

Sauer, Eberhard W., ed. *Sasanian Persia: Between Rome and the Steppes of Eurasia*. Edinburgh University Press, 2017.

Scruton, Roger. *A Short History of Modern Philosophy*. Second Edition. London and New York: Routledge Classics. 2002.

Stausberg, Michael, and Vevaina, Yuhan Sohrab-Dinshaw (editors). *The Wiley Blackwell Companion to Zoroastrianism*. Chichester, West Sussex: John Wiley & Sons, 2015.

Strootman, Rolf. *The Seleucid Era*, Encyclopedia Iranica Online, April 2024.

Tallis, Raymond. *Freedom: An Impossible Reality*. Newcastle upon Tyne: Agenda Publishing. 2021.

Teimourian, Hazhir. *Omar Khayyam: Poet, Rebel, Astronomer*. Stroud, Gloucestershire, England: Sutton. 2007.

----- *The Ultimate Question: in search of God in a godless universe*. London: self-published. 2024.

The Cambridge History of Iran (vol. 2 & 3). Cambridge: CUP, 1983.

The Cambridge Dictionary of Philosophy (2nd ed.). Cambridge: CUP, 1999.

The Encyclopedia of Islam. Brill, Leiden, the Netherlands.

Waters, Matt. *King of the World: The Life of Cyrus the Great*. Oxford: OUP, 2022.

Wilson, Andrew N. *Jesus*. London: Sinclair-Stevenson, 1992.

Xenophon of Athens (430-354 BC). *Anabasis*.

Copyright

ISBN: 9798,2836,3255,1

Published by the Author on Amazon's Kindle Direct Publishing platform.

190

Praise for the author's forthcoming autobiography
To Know that Love Existed

Born in 1940 in the Kurdish region of Iran, Teimourian has had a full and varied life that has brought him into contact with many notable individuals. He was an influential broadcaster and journalist and, in this volume, shares his experiences, as well as his inner thoughts, with us.

Sir Anthony Kenny

Philosopher, former President of the British Academy and Chairman of the British Library

Brilliant. Personal, political, philosophical, erudite. In just over 100,000 words, Teimourian has captured enough of his immensely eventful life to enrapture the reader in his story ... and he raises the most fundamental of questions about human nature.

Sonia Land

Literary agent and former CEO of Harper Collins

Genuinely fascinating. This is a full, rich, sharply-observed panorama, the more interesting in the context of the Middle East and the meeting of cultures which the book explores. ... Hugely absorbing ... I enjoyed the whole experience.

Jonathan Keates

Historian and biographer, Ordine Della Stella d'Italia, former chairman of the Venice in Peril Fund

Everything about Hazhir Teimourian is fascinating: His interesting and improbable family, his exotic and exciting background, the peripeteia of his profession as a journalist and man of letters, the startling range of his friends and acquaintances, the candour with which he recounts his thoughts and passions, the unsurpassed depth of his sensibilities, the transgressive cultural shifts that constitute his life story, and the irresistibly engaging style in which he writes it.

Felipe Fernandez-Armesto

Historian, Knight Grand Cross of the Civil Order of Alfonso the Wise

191

I have known Hazhir Teimourian for a long time, ever since we were neighbours in Limehouse and would go jogging on Sundays. He was a wise and illuminating commentator on the politics of the Middle East. But I find now that there was much about his life that I did not know: his upbringing as a Kurd in a mountainous area of western Iran; his arrival in London to study science; his activities as a critic of the Shah's autocracy that ended in the Islamist takeover of 1979; his immense importance as a journalist and commentator; his years of needing the protection of the police. As he recounts his childhood, career, friendships, loves and marriages, his admiration for England and his philosophical beliefs, one hears his voice throughout: independent-minded, amusing, sagacious. It is a great treat. I have had the utmost pleasure reading it.

Sir Charles Saumarez Smith

Art historian, former Director of the National Gallery and the Royal Academy of Arts

Index

193

195

Printed in Dunstable, United Kingdom